"In her book, [text obscured], Lauren Whitman tenderly addresses parental feelings of inadequacy and perceived failures and guides us to rest in Jesus by sharing stories of him meeting his people's doubts and fears. With honesty and insight, Lauren will help you navigate your parental distress, giving you more confidence in Jesus's sweet grace."

Darby Strickland, Faculty and Counselor, Christian Counseling & Educational Foundation (CCEF); author of *Is It Abuse?* and *Something Scary Happened*

"Lauren's new book, *When Parents Feel Like Failures*, is a fresh breath of gospel encouragement that speaks right to my soul. She reminds me of my Father's love and my Savior's mercy and grace. She reminds me that Jesus does indeed quiet my distressed heart with his love. *When Parents Feel Like Failures* is a book for all parents. Read it and be encouraged."

Christina Fox, Author of *Like Our Father: How God Parents Us and Why That Matters for Our Parenting*

"As I read this book, I noticed the familiar 'churn' of past failures and present inadequacies I have experienced as a parent. But for once, the churn is good, because Lauren Whitman leads us to the Christ of the Gospels who meets real people and real burdens with real love—more than enough to settle the soul."

Andrew Collins, Director of the Certificate Programme, Biblical Counselling UK

"I can think of no better guide for discouraged parents than Lauren, whose tender heart and counseling experience blend so beautifully together in this book. As she helps readers to identify the common emotions, thoughts, and expectations that underwrite feelings of failure, Lauren shows how Jesus consistently offers himself as both a refuge and a rescuer."

Christine Chappell, Certified Biblical Counselor; author of *Midnight Mercies*; *Hope + Help* podcast host, Institute for Biblical Counseling & Discipleship

"If you're an imperfect parent, this book is for you. Instead of offering more 'how-tos' for the already weary parent, this short but wisdom-packed book will offer you a refreshing dose of encouragement wrapped in the freeing gospel of grace."

Sarah Walton, Coauthor of *Hope When It Hurts*,
Together Through the Storms, and *He Gives More Grace*

"*When Parents Feel Like Failures* provides wisdom and gentle guidance for moms and dads weighed down by fear, guilt, shame, or regret. Lauren Whitman's humility as a mom and her saturation in God's Word make this book an effective discipleship guide and a balm for parents' hearts."

Ellen Mary Dykas, Director, Equipping for Ministry to
Women, Harvest USA; counselor; author; Bible teacher

"Lauren Whitman is a wise and gracious counselor who knows Scripture, the noisy hearts of stressed parents, and how to gently connect the two in a way that leads us to rest in the satisfying love of Jesus. My heart was helped by this book, and I enthusiastically recommend it."

Paul Tautges, Pastor; author of *Remade: Embracing Your
Complete Identity in Christ*

"Lauren is a voice of encouragement in the hard moments of parenting. This book gets to the heart of the matter by offering understanding, personal reflection, and scriptural guidance. Both parents and soon-to-be parents will see Jesus, find hope, and gain wisdom from this resource."

Shauna Van Dyke, Founder and biblical counselor,
Truth Renewed Ministries; strategic advisor, The
Association of Biblical Counselors (ABC)

WHEN PARENTS FEEL LIKE FAILURES

HOW JESUS QUIETS OUR DISTRESS

Lauren Whitman

New
Growth
Press

newgrowthpress.com

New Growth Press, Greensboro, NC 27401
newgrowthpress.com

Cover Design: Studio Gearbox, studiogearbox.com
Interior Typesetting/eBook: Lisa Parnell, lparnellbookservices.com

ISBN: 978-1-64507-468-7 (Print)
ISBN: 978-1-64507-469-4 (eBook)

Library of Congress Cataloging-in-Publication Data on file

Printed in the United States of America

31 30 29 28 27 26 25 24   1 2 3 4 5

CONTENTS

Chapter 1

WHERE WE'RE HEADED:
FROM CHURNING
TO QUIETED

Every Friday, a curated batch of the "Funniest Parent Tweets of the Week" is published online. Reading these quips from parents is part of my Friday routine. These funny, sometimes ridiculous, thoughts from parents—about themselves or about their kids—help me to not take myself and my own mishaps so seriously. For example,

> "My wife and I didn't renew our vows, but we did solve our third grader's math problem together."[1]

> "My favorite part about talking to my teens is when they give me direct eye contact, listen intently, nod understandingly, and then take out their AirPods when I finish and say, 'huh?'"[2]

In tweets like these, I can relate to so much of what parents capture. They remind me of the millions of other parents that face the misfortunes, joys, frustrations, and absurdities of parenting. They help me process my own parenting experiences. They make me laugh, sometimes hysterically. But most of all, they remind me that I am not alone in the sometimes wondrous, sometimes chaotic experience of parenting.

THREE GOALS

Let me share the purposes for this book. You may have guessed the first one already: this book exists as a reminder that you, too, are not alone in the wondrous, chaotic experience of parenting. That's the first goal.

This is not a book about *how to* parent. Rather, it is a book for parents that will explore some of what it is like to *be* a parent. More specifically, it is for those who struggle with many hard-to-understand feelings about themselves as parents. If you picked up this book, it's probably because these two words in the title resonated with you: "failure" and "distress." Sadly, these are common feelings that parents wrestle with. You are not alone if you feel that way.

The book's aim is to help you sort out what factors contribute to those feelings. In my experience of being a parent, and as I speak with other parents, I notice that we often feel bad about ourselves. So many parents, in their private thoughts, are burdened by the expectations that they should *be* more, and that they should *be doing* more as parents. When we can't, or when we don't, then we are disappointed with ourselves. We feel deep distress when we can't be the parents we want to be. I will refer to these hard emotions and thoughts throughout the book as *the internal churn* inside of us. The internal churn is the bad feelings and thoughts that constantly roll around in us as we evaluate our parenting day in and day out. Sometimes the churn is loud. This tormenting mix dominates every little interaction with our kids, and the self-condemning thoughts are clear. Sometimes the churn just feels bad, but we can't make out its messages.

This book will help you tease apart what those bad feelings are that churn inside of us. We will deal with four major distressing experiences: fear, guilt, shame, and regret.

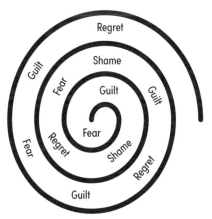

Figure 1. The Churn of Distressing Emotions

And though it can be hard to tease them apart, especially because one experience can lead to another and they can get tangled up together, we will deal with each one separately.

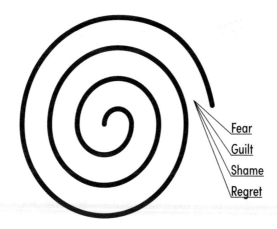

Figure 2. Dealing with Distressing Emotions Individually

As we consider each of the four distressing emotions, you will grow in understanding yourself—both what leads to your internal churn and what keeps it rolling around. That is the second goal.

Once we better understand the true nature of our struggles (goal #2), then we are more aware of what we really need. We can ask for help more knowledgeably. We are ready to seek real forgiveness for real sins. We are better poised to receive real comfort for our real afflictions. We will find that, in order to stop this distressing mix of bad emotions from dominating our experience of parenting, we will need to consider how our Father in heaven responds to some of these common feelings and what leads to them. How does he teach us to understand ourselves? How does he calm and quiet our hearts when the churn roils incessantly? And that brings us to the book's third goal: to take these distressing experiences of parenting, to bring them out into the light of day, and to see how God takes care of them—*how he takes care of us*—when we struggle.

In summary, our three goals are to

1. know you're not alone,
2. grow in self-understanding so that you can accurately name the internal churn of hard feelings you feel as a parent, and
3. receive the Lord's loving care for you in your distressing experiences.

All three of these goals will be worked out again and again in each chapter. The chapters are titled after the four major distressing emotions that make up the internal churn. Along the way, you will meet other parents whose stories will typify these experiences, and I will share some of my own personal experiences as a parent, as well as bring my experiences to bear from my counseling work with distressed parents.

A FIRM FOUNDATION FOR QUIETING OUR DISTRESS

To begin to work toward our three goals, we need a firm foundation. The churn we will talk about is not an experience that is easy to escape. I know this from my personal experience as a mother. To really quiet this churn, we need a voice that speaks *to* us, *about* us. You probably have already discovered that it is not enough to tell yourself that you're a good mother or father. In moments when you're struggling with harsh assessments of your parenting, your own attempts to reassure yourself just aren't persuasive enough. You might try to tell yourself, "I am doing a good job," but you will doubt that just as soon as you think it. We need a voice from outside ourselves. We need that voice to have authority. We need it to be persuasive, and we need to be persuaded by it.

That brings us now to what is perhaps an unexpected place—the book of Zephaniah. It's a book that is easily overlooked in our Bibles. With a mere three chapters, it's hard to even locate it! Zephaniah is one of the so-called minor prophets—and when the prophets are on the scene in the history of God's people, it's because things are really bad. God calls the prophets to bring warnings to the people and to call them to repentance. And though the people are guilty, we learn the love and mercy of God is greater than their guilt. Listen to these words of promise:

> He will rejoice over you with gladness;
>   he will quiet you by his love.
> Zephaniah 3:17

This verse is the theme of our book as we explore God's heart for parents. A churn needs to be quieted. How intriguing that *God's love* is what quiets. That is a truth that deserves further investigation. Let's locate it in its original context and then establish how it becomes an orienting reality that we as God's people have inherited and can cherish.

WE NEED SHELTER

The book of Zephaniah begins with a prophecy that the God who made everything will destroy all that he has made. This will be a reversal of the Genesis creation account. God will break down his created order into chaos. Zephaniah's prophecy is referring to the "Great Day of the Lord," a day of universal judgment for all of mankind. Though Zephaniah goes on in chapter 1 to warn of particular judgment that is coming for the people of Judah in his day, the opening verses go broader. We are all under this broader judgment because all have sinned and all fall short of the glory of God (Romans 3:23). Well, that stirs up a churn in our gut, doesn't it?

I promise we're moving toward good news, but we must start right here—with an accurate understanding of our true condition! We have all messed up in all kinds of ways. We are truly guilty, and God will judge us. These are not particularly welcome thoughts, but this is the truth that comes to us from the authoritative Word of God. Knowing that truth helps us see what our true needs are. If there is to be any hope that we might be spared from judgment, then we will need God to be gracious and merciful to us. It's really our only hope—that God might show us grace. Hold that thought.

Zephaniah follows his pronouncements of guilt and judgment in the pattern of the prophets—with a call to repentance. He pleads for God's people to seek righteousness and humility. If they do, then they "will be sheltered on the day of the LORD's anger" (Zephaniah 2:3 NIV). Only he or she who is sheltered will be able to stand on the Great Day of the Lord.

As for Judah—and the numerous surrounding nations—God's judgment does fall upon them. Each nation crumbles. But even as God brings judgment, he promises that a remnant of Judah would survive (Zephaniah 2:7, 9; 3:9–12). This is grace from God. There is no indication (yet) that Judah has repented and thereby made themselves deserving of a rescue. But the rescue of a remnant is nevertheless foretold. This is the context of the final verses of the book. It's a song of joy—a poem that celebrates God's faithfulness to his people. His people were unfaithful. We have been unfaithful. "All have sinned and fall short," but the book of Zephaniah lands on the note that *God is faithful*.

The poem that ends the book is a song that brims with gladness.

> Sing aloud, O daughter of Zion;
>> shout, O Israel!
> Rejoice and exult with all your heart,
>> O daughter of Jerusalem!
> The Lord has taken away the judgments against
>   you;
>> he has cleared away your enemies.
> The King of Israel, the Lord, is in your midst;
>> you shall never again fear evil.
> On that day it shall be said to Jerusalem:
> "Fear not, O Zion;
>> let not your hands grow weak.
> The Lord your God is in your midst,
>> a mighty one who will save;
> he will rejoice over you with gladness;
>> he will quiet you by his love;
> he will exult over you with loud singing.

What a contrast to the opening verses that spoke fiercely of God's judgment! So if you put the two main messages of Zephaniah together, they say this: God's just judgment is coming *and* God will be faithful to rescue a people for himself—a people he greatly delights in.

Both are true. How can both be true if "all have sinned"? How can God's justice and mercy meet?

They meet on the cross of Jesus Christ. Another judgment day has, in fact, come to pass—and the righteous judgment of God fell upon Jesus. On the cross, God's judgment was poured out on his Son. The Son offered himself, willingly, so that God could rescue a people for himself. God has come close—he is in our midst—through Jesus Christ, mediated through the Spirit that Jesus sent to be with us.

WHAT DOES ZEPHANIAH HAVE TO DO WITH PARENTING?

I wanted those words of promise that God quiets you with his love to come to you situated in their original context, so that you could take a moment to remember and to ponder that God has been faithful to quiet the deepest churn we will ever face. On the Great Day of the Lord, when God will justly judge the whole world, those who have trusted in Jesus will stand righteous and unashamed because Jesus's sacrifice on our behalf has sheltered us. The deepest dread any of us feel—the dread of death and the dread of judgment—we are rescued from. And if God can quiet that churn, then he can quiet the other churns we face in this life, including the ones we face as parents. He is mighty to save—from any terrors we face, both big and small. He saves us—once, for all, and all of the time. Over and over again he proves he is mighty to save and faithful to rescue. That is always the trajectory, and that is always, always the way it goes for God's children who are hidden in Christ. Even if we are faithless, he remains faithful (2 Timothy 2:13). Faithful is who he is. We will count on that as we go through this book.

And still there is more that we can say about what kind of Father he is. In his faithfulness, our God pledged himself to us. "I will be with you," Jesus promised. He will be with us and he will never leave. Remember how Zephaniah captured it: God is in our midst. He is in our midst—and close enough that we can hear his voice.

The authoritative voice that we need to come from outside of us is his voice. Read Zephaniah 3:17 again. His voice is speaking words of rejoicing over us. It's a voice that speaks gently to us—quieting our anxious hearts with the reminder that he loves us and he is for us. He uses his voice—the voice that made the heavens and the earth—to exult over us with loud singing. This is a Father filled with joy and love for his beloved child. It's a love that can't be contained—and so it sings. He sings for you.

Rejoicing, quieting, exulting—this is how our heavenly Father feels toward you. If that is how he feels about us, then we should come to him. "Out of my self to dwell in thy love. . . . Jesus, I come to thee."[3] We should come out of ourselves and into his love. Of course we should. A Father who feels this way about us will want to help us. And he does.

He wants to help you with the fears, the guilt, the shame, and the regrets you wrestle with as a parent. In every struggle, in every distress, he is mighty to save. He is in your midst, and so we will proceed now with every confidence of his love.

He loves you. That is the firm foundation that we will build upon.

QUESTIONS FOR REFLECTION

1. What are your reflections, thoughts, or questions about the message of the book of Zephaniah?

2. What is your initial response to hearing that God delights in you?

3. Where do you struggle with thoughts of parental failure?

4. When you are wrestling with loud, chaotic accusations about your parenting, how does that impact your parenting?

Chapter 2

FEAR IN PARENTING

Here's a key feature of the internal churn: what it churns out are thoughts and feelings that focus on you. It makes evaluations about you—and they never capture you in a fair or accurate light. It's toxic spew. Here are some examples of the churn's output.

> *I am going to mess up my kids.*
> *I should have seen that coming. How could I miss it?*
> *What if others knew how I just yelled at my kids? I'm a monster.*
> *I never wanted to hurt my kids the way my parents hurt me. Am I any better?*
> *I'm a lousy provider.*

This churn is fueled by four emotions: fear, guilt, shame, and regret.

In this chapter, we will look at fear in parenting. As you know, being a parent is really scary! Most parents would agree that being a parent is the biggest responsibility in life. It's a high-stakes endeavor—and parents feel that to their cores. These are people we're talking about. Real, complicated, little human beings that we are called by God to raise and nurture. God wired us to be focused on them and attuned to them. *What do they need? How are they doing? Are they okay? How can I help them? What else can I do? What more can I do?* This care starts the moment we find out we will become parents—and it never ends!

But none of the raising and nurturing that we have to do is straightforward. There is no how-to manual for parents, and even if there was, how could it possibly capture all of the variations of the situations, contexts, and experiences that we encounter? Nothing about parenting is straightforward. How many times have you thought, or how many times have you heard another parent say, "Being a parent is the hardest thing I have ever done"? As a counselor, I have talked to scores of parents; I've heard them say it, and I have said it myself. Being a parent is hard. And for many of us, we find it the hardest thing we have ever been called to do.

Then there is the reality that we live in a world of sorrow and suffering. We have a lot to contend with in parenting. We contend with all of the following challenges and more:

- Our own sins and weaknesses
- Our personal stories of brokenness, including the wounds we carry that still impact us
- Our children's sins and weaknesses
- A broken world where accidents, illness, and disease can and do happen

- A broken society where we are daily bombarded with mixed values and priorities that we must filter and process
- A broken human race made up of a mix of people, some of whom may not be trustworthy, and some who are even inclined to harm children

Of course we are scared. All parents face those challenges listed above. On top of all that, Christian parents have fears about their children's spiritual lives. Will they grow up and be committed Christians? Will they choose to follow what we taught them or go their own way? Will they be saved?

Pause for a moment and think about what it felt like to read those last couple of paragraphs. Notice what is happening in your body. Just writing this has caused my breathing to become shallower, and I feel a little sick to my stomach. I don't like writing what I just wrote because it is hard to acknowledge the real threats that exist. But it's all true, right? Those are realities we contend with, and those are questions we really ask. This life really is high stakes, and we have been entrusted with small people whose lives are precious. Of course we are afraid.

The problem is that we don't always recognize our fear. Notice that the output of the churn of fear is about ourselves. *I am screwing up this parenting thing. Why is this so hard for me?* Let's think about thoughts like these for a moment. Most likely we're not consciously choosing to do so, but why is it that we focus on ourselves? There is more than one answer to that question, but here's one that is especially enlightening: the missionary Elisabeth Elliot noticed that "fear arises when we imagine that everything depends on us." So when we exclusively focus on ourselves, then perhaps we have fallen into that trap of thinking, *it's all on me to make or break this situation that is happening with my child.*

The harsh focus on ourselves is a bit like starting a trial in which we act as our own prosecutors. But we are also the defendants, and the defendants are always losing. The prosecutors have to come down hard, and then maybe the defendants will get a clue. So we come down hard on ourselves. We obsessively evaluate ourselves and try to control what we do, don't do, say, don't say, choose, and don't choose for our kids. This is exhausting and miserable, but it's still a little better than feeling the helplessness that comes when we acknowledge our limited control over our kids and over all that goes into their well-being.

So it is a little twisted, isn't it? There is a logic to it, though, and that's why it is so easy to slip into.

I remember the day I had an insight that helped me first start to identify fear and break free from it. It was during the height of the COVID-19 lockdowns, and, like many families, our kids were not in school, and we were trying to homeschool—trying. But we were having a rough go of it. At the time, my daughter was at a critical age for learning to read, and the problem was that I didn't know how to teach her. I don't have that education or background in elementary-age education. Instead of recognizing that I wasn't equipped for this overwhelming task, I was berating myself for how I was failing to live up to what my daughter needed.

I remember exactly where I was while I was thinking these horrible thoughts when the Spirit broke through my churn. I was walking from the dining room into our living room, and suddenly a new thought came that was so simple: *You are afraid.* How clear! It was a rescue, really. God rescued me in that moment from emotional self-flagellation with that insight. I was afraid. Learning to read is high stakes. It's vitally important and foundational to so much later learning. I had hopes for my daughter—that she'd love to read, become a reader, and be a lifelong learner. But I didn't know how to teach her. Did I deserve to beat myself up for that? No. Was beating myself up for that productive? Not at all.

God's help to me that day put me on a path of establishing a new practice: working to find the words to say something that was more honest than a fear-filled, harsh self-assessment. It wouldn't be honest if I were saying, "You're such a bad mom for not knowing how to do this, Lauren. Why can't you just figure this out?" It wouldn't be honest because that was not what was true about was happening. My struggle in teaching my daughter to read wasn't because I was a bad mom. My struggle was because it's hard to teach kids how to read—and I didn't know how to do it! It's not that I didn't know because of some personal fault or failure, but because it's a specialized area of training. So I had to learn to find truer words for what was I was contending with. In that instance, the words were this: "I'm afraid. This responsibility is falling in my lap because of the pandemic, and I don't know how to do it. And that scares me because of what I hope for my daughter." That's honest. That's true.

And here's the (perhaps unexpected) fruit of this

kind of honest clarity. It actually helps us to respond to the situation more helpfully. If I'm just caught up in chastising myself, then I'm thinking about myself—instead of thinking about my daughter. But if I can honestly acknowledge my fear and acknowledge my own limitations in helping my daughter, then I'm in a much better place to start thinking about and acting productively in this situation.

I am getting a little ahead of myself. I've just named one way we quiet the churn of fear, and perhaps it's counterintuitive, but it's by giving voice to the fear. It's by naming the fear and even naming our limitations in the situation that provokes our fear. It's by then bringing that fear to the Lord in prayer because he is the one who can quiet fears. In our next chapter, we are going to consider just how Jesus does that.

QUESTIONS FOR REFLECTION

1. It can be painful to acknowledge our fears, but avoiding them doesn't make them go away. What makes you afraid in parenting?

2. After you have named your fears, what is something honest you can say to God about them?

3. Consider Elliot's quote: "fear arises when we imagine that everything depends on us." Where do you see yourself imagining that everything with your kids depends on you?

4. What might change if you grew in depending upon the Lord for everything that has to do with your kids?

Chapter 3

HOW JESUS QUIETS FEAR WITH HIS LOVE

How does Jesus help us when we are afraid? Here we will consider Jesus as the one who possesses all power and control. Knowing this truth actually can give us the courage to be honest and acknowledge, "I am not in control of so much that is happening or can happen in my kids' lives, and that scares me." So let's learn how he meets us in that vulnerability. As we consider these two stories about Jesus, let's not focus so much on the similarities between our circumstances and the people in the stories. Instead, let's focus on Jesus. The hope is to see who he is more clearly so we can grow in faith. We want to know that no matter our circumstances and no matter what we fear about our parenting or fear for our kids, he is the one to turn to for help. We are going to see that he wants to help.

Enter Mark 4. When Jesus falls asleep on a boat and a storm rages, the disciples are understandably panicked. Their lives are in danger. Here is how they respond:

And they woke [Jesus] and said to him, "Teacher, do you not care that we are perishing?" And [Jesus] awoke and rebuked the wind and said to the sea, "Peace! Be still!" And the wind ceased, and there was a great calm. He said to them, "Why are you so afraid? Have you still no faith?" And they were filled with great fear and said to one another, "Who then is this, that even the wind and the sea obey him?" (Mark 4:38–41)

Let's notice a few things about this text as we think about the nature of fear, anxieties we have about our children, and what we are to do in the midst of a fear-filled experience. First, finding themselves in a crisis, the disciples accuse Jesus of not caring about them. They set a negative example in so doing, though I don't judge them. I too am tempted to accuse God of a lack of care when situations in my life get hard. When we see our kids suffer or struggle and feel powerless to help, it's also tempting to mistrust God. "God, don't you care about my child?" This question arises, in part, because we cannot control God. We cannot predict what God will do in a given situation. And when it looks like he isn't doing much, then we are tempted to accuse him of being asleep on the job. So it's interesting to see how Jesus handles this accusation on the boat because we don't have direct interactions with him like the disciples did.

Jesus awakes and immediately responds to the crisis. In the gospel accounts, readers are progressively gaining an understanding of who Jesus is and what his mission is. How does this story further our understanding? Jesus simply tells the wind and waves to stop. And they stop. What do we discover from this about who Jesus is? He is the omnipotent God. Someone is in control. And in this story, he uses his power to rescue his disciples. Does he care about them? He cares. He rescues them because he cares.

After Jesus ends the threat of the storm, he then rebukes the disciples and says, "Why are you so afraid? Have you still no faith?" (Mark 4:40). This takes some careful unpacking. Jesus does not rebuke them for being afraid. Their fear is understandable, given the threat of the storm. He rebukes them for not having faith in him. Having been with Jesus, the disciples have good reasons to know who Jesus really is and, therefore, to have faith in him. But they failed to put their faith in him here. Again, I don't judge them. God has proven himself faithful to me, and I still doubt him. We can all see ourselves in the disciples.

Next, notice how their fear changes after Jesus calms the storm. They had been afraid of the storm. But after they see Jesus exercise his authority over the storm, they fear Jesus. This is a good development for them. They have gone from fear of created things (the storm) to fear of the One who created all things. They now experience the fear of the Lord—and that is a good aim for us as parents. To fear the Lord means that we behold God for who he really is. He is the almighty Creator, the one whose voice the wind and waves obey. He is the God who loves us and actively cares for us— and so he rescues us from danger. As we consider who he is, it naturally humbles us. We notice how different he is from us and that leads to humble awe and humble worship of the one who is worthy of our worship. This is what it means to fear the Lord.

HUMILITY WHEN WE ARE AFRAID

Let's continue by considering humility even more closely because it is a key feature of how to deal with our fears and anxieties. The apostle Peter links the concepts of our humility and God's care for us in his letter to suffering people: "Humble yourselves, therefore, under the mighty hand of God so that at the proper time he may exalt you, casting all your anxieties on him, because he cares for you" (1 Peter 5:6–7).

Notice the mention of God's care. There it is again. Does he care? He cares. He cares for you. He cares for your children. The disciples' accusation was flat-out wrong. He does care—he absolutely cares—*and so*, as Peter's logic goes, cast all of your anxieties on him.

Think about that. You have someone to cast your anxieties about your children onto. Someone cares enough about you and about your children to invite you to bring your anxieties to him. He doesn't ask you to solve your own fears or anxieties, or ask you to deal with them on your own. It's not on you to make a raging storm stop. You won't be able to do it. You aren't in control. So cast your cares on him, onto the one who is able to stop a storm, onto the one who *cares* to stop a storm because he cares about you and about your children.

Our final takeaway from Mark 4 is that it would be a fine aim for us to be more like the wind and sea in this story. That sounds funny, but hear me out. The wind and sea hear the Creator's words, and they obey. May we also know who it is who speaks to us. And may we obey him, for he is our Creator. Like the wind and sea, it's a good goal to be controlled by God's voice, to be controlled by the one who made us, and to be controlled by the wisdom he has given us in his Word. We are not in control. But will we be controlled by the one who is? Being controlled by someone is generally perceived as a negative thing. But we are talking about Jesus, who describes himself as "gentle and lowly in heart" (Matthew 11:29). His yoke is easy, and his burden is light. He is the God who wants to take care of you, to ease your burdens, and to be gentle to you. To be controlled by him is to receive his care and his love.

JESUS CARES FOR A FEARFUL FATHER AND HIS DAUGHTER

In the face of our fears in parenting, we are aiming to have faith in Jesus. To increase our faith further, let's meditate on another gospel story in Mark 5. This story involves a father and his daughter. As Jesus's public ministry has begun, people are starting to flock to him for healing. A desperate father seeks Jesus out, evidently believing that Jesus can help: "Then one of the synagogue leaders, named Jairus, came, and when he saw Jesus, he fell at his feet. He pleaded earnestly with him, 'My little daughter is dying. Please come and put your hands on her so that she will be healed and live.' So Jesus went with him" (Mark 5:22–24 NIV).

This is a father with great faith! Jairus knows who to go to. When we are afraid for our children, may we, too, know who to go to. May we come to the one who is in control and whose heart is inclined toward his people. I love the immediacy of Jesus's response. There are no words; the text simply says, "Jesus went." He saw Jairus's desperation, and he went. Jesus responded to the need. As Jesus begins walking toward Jairus's home, he performs another miracle: he heals the woman with the discharge of blood. Then as Jesus and Jairus continue on, someone arrives with bad news. Here is the rest of the story:

> Some people came from the house of Jairus, the synagogue leader. "Your daughter is dead," they said. "Why bother the teacher anymore?"
>
> Overhearing what they said, Jesus told him, "Don't be afraid; just believe."
>
> He did not let anyone follow him except Peter, James and John the brother of James. When they came to the home of the synagogue leader, Jesus saw a commotion, with people crying and wailing loudly. He went in and said to them, "Why all this commotion and wailing? The child is not dead but asleep." But they laughed at him.
>
> After he put them all out, he took the child's father and mother and the disciples who were with him, and went in where the child was. He took her by the hand and said to her, *"Talitha koum!"* (which means "Little girl, I say to you, get up!"). Immediately the girl stood up and began to walk around (she was twelve years old). At this they were completely astonished. (Mark 5:35–42 NIV)

There is so much comfort for us as parents in this miracle!

Jairus's daughter has died. Those who meet Jairus on the road to inform him suggest that he should no longer "bother" Jesus to come. But Jesus lets himself be bothered.

Parents, bother Jesus.

Bother Jesus because he cares about your children—and, of course, it is not actually a bother to him at all. When Jesus hears this comment, he turns to Jairus and encourages him to not be afraid. Jairus's fear has come true, and if anyone said to him, "Don't be afraid," it would be cruel. But Jesus is not just anyone. He is God. He is the God who lets himself be "bothered" by scared parents who are coming to him on behalf of their vulnerable children.

"Don't be afraid; just believe," Jesus told Jairus. Instead of fear, have faith. Will we "just believe" that the Jesus we have called upon is going to come through for our children? Lord, help us believe!

Seeing what Jesus does next in this story helps us believe. Jesus does not turn around because Jairus's daughter has died. He continues to walk toward her. And when he arrives at their home, he does what is impossible for man, but what is possible for God: he raises her from death to life.

One of the greatest fears parents have is the death of their children. This has happened to Jairus. But Jesus is there, and so the story doesn't end with death, but with life. The resurrection of this little girl is a foretaste of the great resurrection that is coming. Death has lost its sting for all who have trusted in Jesus. We are promised life after death. What is impossible for man is possible for God. This is why we put our faith and trust *in him*. He is able to bring life after death; this story shows us it's possible. More than that, he *wants* to help us in all of our afflictions. And so he helps.

What Jesus does for Jairus is the message of Zephaniah being worked out in real people's lives in new, glorious ways. He is merciful, and he mercifully quiets all of the churning we will ever face. He quiets the churn of death for Jairus's daughter. And, as we said in chapter 1, if he can quiet the churn of death and judgment, then he can quiet all of the lesser ones we and our children face.

HOW JESUS QUIETS OUR FEARS

Let's put together all that we have gleaned from these two stories in Mark to find an answer to this question: How does Jesus quiet our fears?

- Jesus quiets our fears by assuring us that he cares.
- Jesus quiets our fears by using his power on our behalf. He is a rescuer.
- Jesus quiets our fears by inviting us to fear him—to see who he really is and to put our faith in him because of who he is.
- Jesus quiets our fears by inviting us to humble ourselves. We are not in control and so, in humble faith, we place our trust in him, the one who is in control.
- Jesus quiets our fears by inviting us to believe in him. To believe that he is God, that he is with us, and that he is ever inclined to help us.

QUESTIONS FOR REFLECTION

1. A fine aim for us as Christian parents is to have an increasing faith in Jesus. Jesus commends those who believe in him. One way for our faith to grow is to watch what Jesus is like in the gospel stories. Read another gospel story—Mark 9:14–29. In the story, we see another father coming to Jesus for help with his child. What stands out to you about Jesus in this story? What is something that you observe about Jesus that can calm your fearful heart for your children?

2. In the Mark 9 story, the father cries out, with tears, "I believe; help my unbelief!" We all have unbelief in us. In moments of desperation, I invite you to borrow this father's words. They are so honest. What are some situations in your parenting right now in which you need to cry out to Jesus, "Lord, I believe. Help my unbelief!"

A PRAYER FOR FEARFUL PARENTS

God, I am afraid of so much when it comes to my kids.

Increase my faith that you care for them and that you care for me.

Help me to grow in humility and trust you with what is out of my control.

Chapter 4

GUILT IN PARENTING

Guilt is the second challenging experience that we will explore. To understand guilt, we must first distinguish between true guilt and false guilt. Let's start there.

First, true guilt is guilt before God. God created us as moral creatures with the capacity to choose good or evil. When we choose evil, God made it that we experience guilt. In other words, true guilt comes after we have sinned. God allows us to feel guilt, and it is meant to function as a type of alert. It alerts us of the need to do something important and necessary: confess to God and to those we have hurt, and repent, asking forgiveness from both God and the people we hurt. Of course, as sinners, we all inevitably have sinned against our children. There is no denying it: there are times when we are impatient, unkind, indifferent, dishonest, and petty toward our children. When we are, and we feel guilty, that feeling is alerting us to the reality that we have sinned against our children and against God.

Do any of these stories sound familiar?

Stephanie feels guilty when she hears her older son yell at her younger son. He sounds exactly the way she sounded two hours earlier when she yelled at him. Her failure to model a gracious response has resulted in her son failing to give a gracious response to his brother.

When Jackson's seven-year-old daughter says to him in frustration, "You never want to play with me. You're always on your phone!" Jackson knows she's not wrong. His phone tracks his usage: at 11 a.m. he's already had four hours of screen time. He's not surprised his daughter noticed, and he feels guilty.

When Jared hears his seventeen-year-old son make a sexually suggestive comment about an attractive woman, he feels guilty. His mind quickly flashes to the two times in the past year that he has made objectifying comments about a woman's appearance in front of his son.

As we will see, Christians have a place to go when we feel guilty. Guilt can be resolved. We'll get to that in the next chapter.

In contrast to true guilt, we experience what I will call "false guilt" after committing a nonmoral choice. This experience is not as straightforward as true guilt, so we will spend more time unpacking it. I'll begin with a scenario to help us consider false guilt.

After a long day, you feel too exhausted to cook, and you heat up some frozen chicken nuggets for your kids. But you feel guilty for it. This experience of guilt is not true guilt. You have not sinned against God or your kids by serving nuggets. You might feel bad about it, but this experience of guilt is deceptive; it is not accurately capturing what you have done. It is not alerting you to a true failure or a moral breach. In recent years, the phrase *mom guilt* has become a part of our vernacular—and indeed it is a common experience of many moms.[1] Mom guilt can be best categorized as false guilt. Of course dads feel false guilt, too. Why do so many parents struggle with this? That's a good question! Let's explore some possibilities to better understand this experience.

Our human limitations lead to false guilt. We feel false guilt when we bump against our human limitations. We each have our own limitations. Let's go back to the frozen chicken nuggets example. You had a long day. You worked. You are now tired. You have limited time to feed your kids before bedtime. These are limitations you are facing because you are a created being living within time and bodily constraints. This is why the concept of *supermom* is so cruel. The term comes from Superman, of course, who was a superhero, a hero who lived *beyond* human bodily constraints. To put supermom expectations on mere moms (or dads) is to be set up to experience false guilt because we all have limitations.

Each of us also has our own set of personal limitations. Mine are different from yours. That reality is why it is important to resist comparing ourselves to other parents. Sometimes we see something good in other parents, and we feel false guilt that we do not provide what they provide. But none of us is the same, and our limitations differ from theirs, so it's not wise or kind to compare ourselves to them. Not only that, but it also could lead us to compete with other parents in our hearts. We might try to do what they do, but with a competitive motive that seeks to prove we are better than other parents in some way. We might try to find ways to feel good about ourselves by looking down on others.

A perceived failure to live up to standards leads to false guilt. We all live by standards. Maybe these are self-imposed standards. Perhaps they are ones that you have witnessed and admired in others and then placed on yourself—for example, maybe your parents consistently fed you home-cooked meals, which you appreciated. It's helpful to recognize this standard that was modeled for you and that you wanted to adopt, and to recognize that you are comparing yourself in this area to your parents without taking into account the ways your set of circumstances and limitations differ. But recognizing this can help you understand some of the guilty feelings you get when your kids eat frozen chicken nuggets. If the standard is home-cooked meals, and you didn't cook, then you have failed to meet that standard, and false guilt follows.

You may also have standards that are placed upon you by your spouse, by your family, or by your community. These standards may reflect truly good ideas, but the problem comes when others view that idea as the only good option, and then you evaluate yourself as failing if you do not live up to it or see it that way. We feel false guilt when we make a choice that is morally acceptable, but different from what others around us think we should choose. We might sense that others are judging us for that choice we made, and this, too, can lead to false guilt. For example, within the American Christian community, many parents have the choice of how to educate their children. They can choose home-school, public school, or private school. If a good majority of your community favors one of these choices over another and holds strong opinions that their choice is the "best" choice, then you might feel false guilt when you choose differently for your child. It can feel as if you have failed because you have not measured up to a community-held standard of what schooling choice is best.

The society and culture you live in will also have standards of what makes a "good" or "bad" parent. What standards have you adopted from the culture you live in? What are some characteristics of the parenting values that the society you live in upholds?

In the modern, Western society that I live in, the ideal model of parenting is called *intensive parenting*. Research shows that across both socioeconomic and cultural lines, there is wide agreement among parents that this is the ideal way to parent. Author Sharon Hays describes intensive parenting as "child-centered, expert-guided, emotionally absorbing, labor-intensive, and financially expensive."[2] Hays notes that all societies develop norms for parenting, and that it's difficult not to view your society's norms as *the only correct way* to parent. I will not focus here on the strengths and weaknesses of intensive parenting; rather, I raise the subject to alert you to the need to recognize the sociohistorical moment you find yourself in because that moment can contribute to false guilt.

Just to go one layer deeper into the "child-centered" feature of intensive parenting, consider these data points about the amount of time that parents spend with their children:

- In 1965, during an era when women were not yet a regular presence in the workforce, mothers spent 3.7 *fewer* hours per week providing childcare than they did in 2008, even though, in 2008, women worked almost three times as many paid hours.
- Fathers spent over three times as many hours with their children in 2008 than they did in 1965.[3]
- The word *parent* (a noun) began to be used as a verb in 1970. It "entered common usage as something one could *do* all day long."[4]
- Women today spend 17.5 hours per week on housework versus 32 hours per week in 1965. "But they have become domestic scientists in another way: now they're parenting experts, and they spend more time with their children than their mothers ever did." Notice, too, a change in nomenclature between these two generations. Women used to call themselves "housewives," but now refer to themselves as "stay-at-home moms." This change "reflects the shift in cultural emphasis: the pressures on women have gone from keeping an immaculate *house* to being an irreproachable *mom*."[5]
- Fathers, too, feel the effect of current cultural priorities. The Families and Work Institute found that today's fathers "work longer hours than their counterparts without kids" and that

men are more apt to experience work–family conflict than women. In other words, dads work longer hours, motivated presumably to provide economically for their children, *and* they feel the tension of working longer hours because it means less time with their kids. Ellen Galinsky, head of the Families and Work Institute, suspects fathers today have had a shift in *internal* priorities: "They don't want to be stick figures in their children's lives."[6] Longer work hours increase the risk of being a stick figure, yet there's the pressure to provide, so they work those longer hours. Do you see the conundrum for the modern dad?

I share all of this with you because we tend to live like a fish in water, taking for granted the water (i.e., cultural norms) in which we live. We all live within certain sociological, societal, and historical contexts, and we are impacted by what is in the water, so to speak. What we assume is "normal" about our experience as parents isn't how parents have always thought about or lived out their roles as parents. Understanding what has been deemed "normal" for you can help you contextualize some of the pressures you face.

Modern parents also live in the age of information. We are swimming in a sea of information. Because of the internet, never before in history have people had access to so much information. Never before have there been so many resources available for parents about how to parent. And the theories on parenting keep evolving, and your choices keep increasing.

Here's an experiment. Read the questions that follow and notice how going through the list makes you feel.

- Are you a tiger mom or a dolphin dad?
- Have you tried elephant parenting?
- What about a free-range approach?
- Have you heard of therapeutic parenting yet?
- Have you read about how parents in other cultures raise their kids and incorporated the best of their approaches into your own?
- What style is best for your kid: Helicopter? Snowplow? Panda?
- What style jibes with your instincts: Attachment? Permissive? Authoritarian?
- Is it okay to go with your instincts, or should you ignore your inclinations in favor of the advice you read from experts in child development?
- Which approach produces the best outcomes for children as they grow into adulthood?

I'll stop there. How does reading that list make you feel? It's overwhelming, isn't it?

Parents are drowning in a sea of information *about parenting*.

All of the theories and styles of parenting mentioned above really exist—and being reminded of all that you could be reading up on gets that churn going inside of us. These are our kids—nothing matters more to us—and so we feel fear that if we don't have the information we could have, then we may be doing them harm. We feel false guilt when we know there is more information out there that we could consume, but then we hit our limitations again and find we don't have the bandwidth to access all of the content that is at our fingertips.

As I said, it helps to know what you're swimming in, because then you can evaluate those values, emphases, standards, and priorities more clearly. One of the values of the modern world is having and gaining more knowledge through information. This value extends to the realm of parenting and can leave parents feeling ill equipped as we realize that there is so much more we could know but don't know. And this again leads to false guilt. The guilt of thinking, *I should be reading more, I should be learning more*, or *I don't want my kids to suffer because I was ignorant of something I should have known.* The problem is that there is always more to read and always more to learn, so when have you done enough? Even asking that question might make us feel guilty. How can it ever be enough when we're talking about our kids? It seems like we can't get off the hook because that will mean we're not doing all we can for our kids. And if we're not reading and learning all we can for our kids' sake, then are we bad parents?

Can you see how a societal value on information gets the cycle of false guilt churning?

WHEN TRUE AND FALSE GUILT INTERTWINE

Let me make one final point about true and false guilt: they can roll around together, and sometimes it can be hard to discern what is true guilt and what is false. So you will have to slow down and tease apart what is happening. Here is an example.

Ben is a first-time dad to a baby boy. Four months into being a parent, he is astonished at the changes to his and his wife's lifestyle that a baby has introduced! He misses the leisurely walks and talks he had with his wife, their dates, and their ability to sleep in on a Saturday. Ben's brother and his wife live nearby and they don't have kids. Ben finds that he feels jealous of them, and he now has a hard time hearing about what they're up to because it highlights his struggle with his loss of independence.

Ben feels guilty. He feels like a bad dad for missing his "old life" and like a bad brother for harboring jealousy. What's going on here?

Let's tease it apart.

Remember true guilt comes from a moral failure, a choice against God. Is feeling gobsmacked by the realities of parenting an example of moral failure? Or feeling sadness for a season of life that has ended because a new baby has arrived? No. To feel guilt for those feelings is false guilt. Ben is in the midst of a major life transition, and it's normal to feel overwhelmed as he is learning what his new role requires. It's also normal that he feels a sense of loss for what life was like before their son arrived. There was a real sweetness to his and his wife's lifestyle that is truly not the same anymore. A new baby is, of course, a blessing, and there is a new kind of sweetness. But that doesn't erase the hardship of losing something else that was good.

Even so, Ben's sin is tangled up with the natural feelings of loss that often accompany a big change. To jealously covet his brother's lifestyle *is* a moral failure. So it's not wrong to feel the losses Ben feels, but what he is doing in response to those feelings is wrong. He must find another direction to go in his heart—another way to deal with the feelings of loss. A faithful response to loss is to grieve, to lament, and to give thanks to God for the good gifts he gave then and now. A faithful response to jealousy is to repent of it and commit to a godly way forward.

What could that way forward look like? Ben can ask God for help when he feels overwhelmed with the responsibilities of fatherhood. He can commit to battle the jealousy when it crops up—to actively push back against it. It can help if he has these categories of true and false guilt because then he can accurately reframe for himself what is happening in those moments. "I'm in the midst of a major transition, and I miss some aspects of what life was like. God, help me to resist wanting what is not mine. Help me to be present in what you call me to do today, and thank you that in all seasons of my life, you are steady. You are faithful and true. Make me like you."

From Ben's story, and from all of the discussion in this chapter of both true and false guilt, we have proven, once again, that we need a strong Savior both because of the complexities we face and because our personal needs are so great. The good news is that Jesus is both mighty to save and mighty to rescue. He is our remedy for both true guilt and false guilt. In our next chapter, we will see how Jesus's love quiets guilt.

QUESTIONS FOR REFLECTION

1. What sins have you committed against your children that cause you to experience true guilt?

2. It's helpful to think about what standards of parenting you have adopted and where they come from. This will help you better understand yourself in preparation for instances when you experience false guilt. Take some time to think about that and list out those standards.

The standard	Where it comes from

3. Imagine your friend comes to you and says, "I'm really struggling because my daughter has a friend whose mom is a preschool teacher and she is so good with kids. She just has this way with them and they adore her. I always feel so awkward around kids, including my own. I am not this playful, happy-go-lucky person—never have been—and I feel so guilty that I can't be more natural with my kids like this other mom."

How would you tease apart what is happening? Where is there false guilt in this situation?

4. As a follow up to #3, do you ever feel tempted to compare yourself to other parents and use them as your measuring stick for how you measure up as a parent? How is doing so unkind to yourself?

Chapter 5

HOW JESUS QUIETS GUILT WITH HIS LOVE

Just as we considered true guilt and false guilt separately in the previous chapter, so we will consider them separately here.

HOW JESUS QUIETS TRUE GUILT

Enter the apostle Peter. Jesus calls Peter and his brother Andrew to be his disciples in Matthew 4. The brothers were fishermen, and when Jesus invites them to "fish for people," "at once they left their nets and followed him" (Matthew 4:20 NIV). You have to admire their lack of hesitation in responding to Jesus's call. Peter's journey in following Jesus, however, does not turn out to be a straight line of unwavering devotion. Throughout the gospels, we see that Peter has a mix of faith and fervor, of lapses and letdowns. A mix—like us. But through Peter's foibles, his ups and downs, we see a steady Jesus who loves him without wavering. We see Jesus, who shows us God's heart of forgiveness for us when we are guilty of true failures.

Peter is, of course, infamous for denying Jesus three times. Jesus had predicted his denial, and even told Peter about it ahead of time. Peter doesn't believe Jesus. He says to Jesus, "Even if all fall away on account of you, I never will" (Matthew 26:33). Jesus knew better: "Truly I tell you . . . this very night, before the rooster crows, you will disown me three times" (v. 34).

But Peter couldn't fathom this. He insisted, "Even if I have to die with you, I will never disown you" (v. 35). When Peter does in fact deny Jesus three times, it seems he is able to understand what he has done against his God. Peter's response? After Peter's third denial, Jesus looked straight at him and Peter "wept bitterly" (Luke 22:62). Remember that Jesus gave the name, Peter, to him in John 1:42, and this name is a version of the word "rock," *petros*. But by his denial, Peter is not at all like a rock. In the terror of the events leading up to Jesus's death, Peter crumbles and is weak. We understand why he cried these bitter tears, and it's easy to imagine the self-disgust he likely felt because of what he did against his Lord. In the wake of his failure, he returned to fishing for actual fish, instead of carrying forward with his call to fish for men. He walked away from his call.

But the resurrected Jesus seeks him out. After a night of fishing with no luck, Jesus calls out to Peter from the shore. He calls him "friend": "Friends, haven't you any fish?" (John 21:5). Do you see the direction Jesus is going after Peter's failure? It's grace. It's all grace— grace to come and find him by the sea, grace to call him friend after Peter failed to be a good friend to him, and then even more—grace upon grace. Three times, Jesus allows Peter to reassert his love for him. It's a reversal of

Peter's denials. Jesus then reinstates his call upon Peter's life. Jesus says to him, "Follow me!" (John 21:19).

In this interaction, we see how Jesus quiets our guilt. His grace quiets our guilt. Jesus has decided that our sins and failures don't have to be the end of our story. And so Jesus seeks out guilty people. He offers new chances. He calls us his friends. He establishes us by his love, not by our merit. In a poem about Peter, author Malcolm Guite writes,

> I love the way [Jesus] chose to name you,
> before you knew how to deserve the name.[1]

Jesus named Peter "the rock" before he deserved the name. In fact, after Jesus named him that, Peter proved that he *didn't* deserve the name! I can relate to that as a parent. In my guilt over real sins and failures in my parenting, sometimes I feel undeserving of the name "mom." But Jesus chose this calling in my life, and he enters into the story of my parenting with me. He doesn't call me to it and then leave me to it. He is with me. And for the times I blow it, he seeks me out. He offers new chances. He is a friend to me. He establishes me by his love, not by my merit.

How does he establish guilty sinners? He enables us to stand after failure by offering a way forward. We have choices before us. We can follow him! Confession and repentance—that is the way he gives us to follow him after we have sinned. We repent and confess to God and to those we have sinned against. We can confess our sins against our children to our children.

Let's go back to the parents from the previous chapter. Stephanie can both confess her harshness to her son and call him to repentance: "When I hear you speak to your brother like that, I hear myself and how I spoke to you earlier. I was angry, and I was harsh with you. I was wrong. Will you forgive me? It is also wrong for you to speak to him like that. Let's pray now, confess our harshness to God, and ask him for help to grow in speaking to one another in loving, kind ways."

Jackson can confess his preoccupation with his phone and offer reassurance to his daughter: "I was on my phone too much this morning, and I'm sorry. I've put it away, and I will ask God for help to resist scrolling. But I love you more than anything, and I love playing with you! What would you like to play?"

Jared can confess to his son and call him to repentance: "Son, it is not respectful to speak about women in that way. I have made similar comments before, and that was wrong of me. Please forgive me for that, and let's both commit to speaking in ways that reflect that a woman's value has nothing to do with what she looks like."

We can live out the call of our faith in front of our children. We can model repentance to our children. We can model dependence on the Father to live righteously. We can model that we are real sinners who have been offered a real remedy. The real remedy is the forgiveness of sins. Jesus, the Lamb of God, offered himself as a sacrifice so that this remedy could be extended to us. Jesus's death and resurrection is the historical basis of our faith. It is our assurance that we are forgiven. And now? Now nothing can separate us from God's love. Listen to the apostle Paul's logic:

> Who will bring any charge against those whom God has chosen? It is God who justifies. Who then is the one who condemns? No one. Christ Jesus who died—more than that, who was raised to life—is at the right hand of God and is also interceding for us. (Romans 8:33–34 NIV).

No charges are held against you. No one can condemn you. It is God who justifies you. Right now Jesus is interceding for you. Do you sense how there is no room for guilt in light of those truths? Instead, it naturally follows that in the freedom resulting from that lack of guilt, we are free to confess our real sins and seek forgiveness. For it is God—*God!*—who justified you! I love the way he chooses to save us before we know how to deserve the honor. Forgiveness of sins is God's gift to you. His forgiveness establishes you in his love.

May we live in gratitude for that, but do so knowing that, like Peter, we will waver. In our walk with Jesus, and within our calling as parents, we will live out a mix of faith and fervor, a mix of real lapses and letdowns. But through our ups and downs, may we see Jesus—the steady one—who does not waver in how he loves us.

In our guilt, we are tempted to look at ourselves—to despair because we have botched it, to come to even hate ourselves for how we have disappointed those we love the most. But, as Robert Murray M'Cheyne puts it, this is what we must learn instead: "Learn much of the Lord Jesus. For every look at yourself, take ten looks at Christ. He is altogether lovely. Such infinite majesty, and yet such meekness and grace, and all for sinners, even the chief!"[2]

Will you practice looking ten times at Jesus every time you look at yourself and see your sin? He is altogether lovely. When guilt churns, look at his meekness and grace—it's who he is. And his meekness and grace are all for sinners. So learn much of him. May he be what you know the best. Of all that you know to be sure and true in life, may you know that you can be surest of him. Look at him. You will see how he loves—and keeps loving—even the chief of sinners.

HOW JESUS QUIETS FALSE GUILT

In the previous chapter, we considered two common sources of parental false guilt: limitations and standards. Let's consider what God has to say about each of them.

To be human is to be limited. Somehow we have to accept that it was God's choice to make us limited *and* that we are wonderfully made! Our limitations are not an oversight or an accident; they are by design. If they are according to God's design, then they are good.

The challenge, of course, is that sometimes they don't feel good. We feel that churn of false guilt when we perceive how our personal limitations impact or even hinder our children. I don't have an easy answer that solves that dilemma, but there are biblical truths that point us in the direction of how to think well about limitations. We've already identified one: God has chosen to make us limited creatures. Let's build from there.

Another way to say we are limited is to say we are weak. To be human is to have weaknesses. Weaknesses do not fall under the category of sin. Here's an example of a weakness: someone might have no sense of how to read a map. But someone else might have an innate sense of direction. Another weakness is if someone has no knack for technology. Sitting in front of a computer and trying to figure out how it works is like asking the person to fly a rocket to the moon. But for others navigating technology is a strength. We each have our own mixtures of strengths and weaknesses. But here is the good news: no one is an island. God means for us to live among one another, to offer our strengths to one another, and to build up one another in our weaknesses. "For the body does not consist of one member but of many" (1 Corinthians 12:14). For believers, we are each one member of a larger body of people, and more than that, we "all belong to each other" (Romans 12:4–5 NLT). God provides for us in our weaknesses by giving us to one another.

What implications does that have for parenting? We can ask for help from each other! Parenting is challenging, on-the-job training, and we are constantly pushed to our personal limits. But if I know I'm just one member, and I also know that I'm free from the expectation to function as if I'm the whole body when I'm not, then that freedom can move me toward others for help. If I have also taken a competitive stance toward other parents, then my sin has entangled me, and I need to repent of competing with other parents. If my motive is love, instead of competition that tries to find ways to feel good about myself, then I appreciate that strengths exist outside of me. I commit to the practice of finding delight in our differences. I appreciate the goodness of differences because they can foster community and interdependence. My children will be blessed and helped by this community and interdependence. I can't be their all in all—and God doesn't call me to be. One of the characteristics and values of modern Western culture is self-sufficiency, but this runs counter to God's vision for how his people are to live life together! We are free from feeling bad or inferior to others because of our limitations and weaknesses, and we are invited to partake of all the gifts and strengths available to us within the body of Christ (1 Peter 4:10). Parents will be blessed as they grow in asking for help.

If you are facing a new challenge with one of your children, ask one or two trusted people for their thoughts. They don't even have to be fellow parents; I have received so many good ideas from people who are not parents. If you tend to struggle with time management and are concerned with what you are modeling to your kids, ask one or two people whose discipline in this area you admire to share what works for them. Ask them to pray for you to grow in this area. And pray for yourself! "God, help me remember to make a schedule for today's activities and help me stick to it."

With these recommendations, I want to note that I am encouraging growth and strengthening of our weaknesses—not perfection. Do not set a self-imposed standard of perfection; you will only set yourself up for more frustration and feelings of failure if you do that.

God has determined that we grow over time, so accept the time spent in the challenges of parenting as a God-given opportunity for growth.

Notice, too, how this discussion on limitations naturally helps us recalibrate our standards. If we all have limitations and weaknesses, then we can accept—without guilt—that we will (of course) live within them, and that we will (of course) fall short of so many standards. So how, then, should we think about standards? Once we've identified the ones that exist for us, how do we think through what to do about it? I think it's helpful to consider the ideas contained within the standard and evaluate those ideas on their own merit. So try to set aside for a moment the value that your culture or a particular person has assigned to the ideas, and evaluate the ideas based on their own merit. From there, know that you have the freedom to decide, to pray about, to ponder, or to discuss if that idea can or should find its way into your parenting. And one major consideration for if it can or should find its way into your parenting is if the idea falls within your limits and reflects your strengths and weaknesses!

For example, let's go back to the standard of home-cooked meals. It would be wise to consider questions like these: can you realistically achieve this every night, considering the time, energy, and money it will require? Do you have the support in place from your spouse to carry this out? If you are a single parent, then, no, you won't have another adult to support you in this task, and that should be a significant consideration for whether this idea is viable. Who will watch the kids while you're in the kitchen? Who will do the dishes?

These are real decisions that real people will have to make. It's easy for a standard to exist in our minds, but are we actually able to realistically meet this standard in this season of life? Each of us is an individual, and God knows very well the contours of our capabilities. "He knows our frame, and remembers that we are dust" (Psalm 103:14).

Apply this same kind of reasoning to the fact that we live in an age of information. How can we wisely think about our proximity to all of the information that is available to us about parenting? First, common sense leads us to acknowledge that there is more to read out there than any of us could ever read. That's an acknowledgment of our limits. You can't read it all. Second, just because you have so much you *could* access doesn't mean you *should*. God encourages his people to number our days, so that we may gain a heart of wisdom (Psalm 90:12 NIV). Our days are numbered; we live within constraints. So live like that is true.

For some of you, though, you might want to learn and read more about parenting, and I commend you in that! So set reasonable goals for yourself. Set limits that are wise. Perhaps set a goal: *this year I will read two books on parenting.* If two books are too much for this year, read one. The point is that you are free to choose or not to choose, and it is wise to consider the full picture of your responsibilities, bandwidth, and time commitments. Choose to access information within the particularities of your life and your actual ability and availability. God is utterly realistic about who we are, and we are invited to have that same kind of understanding about ourselves and our situation. And with

that invitation comes the freedom to walk in this truth:
I am a real person with real limits.

And just as our limitations can nudge us toward
interdependence on the body of Christ, so can our
weaknesses nudge us toward dependence on the Lord.
God's kingdom is unlike what we are used to. In his
kingdom, the last are first. The leaders are those who
serve. To live, you must die to yourself. And, for our
discussion, when you are a weak member of God's
kingdom, then you are strong. When the apostle Paul
pleaded with God to deliver him from his weakness—
the "thorn in his flesh"—this is what God said: "My
grace is sufficient for you, for my power is made perfect
in weakness" (2 Corinthians 12:9).

Upon receiving that understanding from God,
Paul goes on to say: "Therefore I will boast all the more
gladly about my weaknesses, so that Christ's power
may rest on me. That is why, for Christ's sake, I delight
in weaknesses, in insults, in hardships, in persecutions,
in difficulties. For when I am weak, then I am strong"
(2 Corinthians 12:9–10 NIV).

So when we feel the churn of false guilt because we
know we are weak and limited, when we see that we
have failed again to live up to certain standards, Jesus
quiets that churn by saying, "My grace is sufficient for
you." This is a truly unexpected message.

It's not, "I expected more from you."

It's not, "I'm disappointed that this is so hard for
you."

It's not, "You really need to put in more effort.
What you're doing is not cutting it."

That's not what he says when he encounters our weaknesses and limitations. There's no accusation or condemnation. He does speak. But he says something about himself: "My grace is sufficient for you."

His grace is sufficient. For *you*. Parents need to listen to him say that to us again and again. We need to let that message find its way deep in our souls until our inner logic is more accustomed to thinking, "I will boast all the more gladly about my weaknesses, so that Christ's power may rest on me." From there, this becomes a prayer we can each pray: "God, would Christ's power come and rest on me as I parent?" Wouldn't it be amazing if that happened? Instead of endless reaching, or striving, or trying harder to meet standards, it's a plea for Christ's power to rest on you. God doesn't ask you to come up with the power on your own. Instead, we learn to depend on his power.

To pull the chapter all together, here are two summary statements to leave with:

Jesus quiets true guilt by declaring that no charge is held against you and that he is interceding for you now—now!—as you seek to live anew.

Jesus quiets false guilt by providing his sufficient grace for our weaknesses.

QUESTIONS FOR REFLECTION

1. In the beginning of his second epistle, Peter writes, "May grace and peace be multiplied to you in the knowledge of God and of Jesus our Lord" (2 Peter 1:2). What connection is he making between the experience of peace and the knowledge of God and Jesus?

2. Thinking again about Peter's personal story with the Lord, how does his statement in 2 Peter 1:2 reflect his own story? How did Jesus quiet his guilty churn?

3. Read Peter and Jesus's interaction in John 13:6–10. What is the meaning of Jesus washing his disciples' feet, and how does it connect to our conversation about how Jesus quiets true guilt?

4. What are your personal takeaways from this chapter as you consider your unique experience of guilt in parenting?

A PRAYER FOR GUILTY PARENTS

Father, thank you that your grace is sufficient.

It is sufficient for me, and I receive it with gratitude.

Help me to recognize my limitations.

Teach me to live in dependence on your power as I parent today.

Chapter 6

SHAME IN PARENTING

Shame is the next difficult experience we will deal with. First let me distinguish briefly between guilt and shame. Though this certainly doesn't cover all of the nuances, here is a way to think about the differences:

- True guilt arises because of something sinful I have done.
- Shame arises because of something about who I am. This conclusion about who I am can be informed by what I have done. But whatever it is that I have done defines who I am.

It's the difference between *something I have done* and *who I am*.

If a parent occasionally loses her temper with her kids, then she will feel true guilt. If she loses her temper every day, and feels she can't control it, even when she tries, then she will feel true guilt *and* shame. If it happens every day, losing her temper is characteristic of her parenting. In that case, it's harder to think this is just something she does. If she does it all the time, and if she can't stop herself, then it is a feature of who she is as a person. And knowing that sinful anger is wrong and harmful, this mom feels ashamed. Shame connected to a sin struggle often comes from sin that extends over time, is repeated, and has been challenging to get a handle on.

People can experience shame not only because of something deficient about who they are as people, but also because of something evil that was done to them by someone else. Or shame can arise if someone has an unwanted difference that makes that person feel set apart, such as a disfigurement or disability.

For parents, shame occurs usually because of something that they have done—or not done—that impacts their children and therefore impacts how they see themselves as parents. Or it can be due to something about themselves that they see as deficient or lacking that negatively impacts their children in some way. Let's look at these first two sources of shame, along with examples of each, so that we can more clearly put our fingers on what this experience of shame in parenting is like. Then, I'll describe a third source of shame.

Parents feel shame because of a consequential moral failure that has a deep impact on the shape of their parenting

Anna became a mom at the age of seventeen to a baby boy she named Daniel. She married Daniel's father when she was eighteen. By the time Anna was twenty, she was divorced and learning how to provide for her toddler as a single mom after her husband abandoned them. Since then, Daniel's father has shown little interest in his son and has not seen him for ten years.

Being divorced in itself can be a cause of shame. Divorce reflects brokenness. No matter the cause, feelings of personal failure accompany this experience. And society even has a name for you: you are a *divorcée*. You are identified with this brokenness—and that causes shame.

But shame goes even deeper for Anna because she is also a mom. Now in her thirties, Anna has remarried. She and her husband have had two children together. Anna's firstborn son, Daniel, is now a teenager and struggles to feel that he fits in with his mom's "new" family. Anna has tried to create connections between Daniel, Daniel's siblings, and her husband, but her son persistently feels like an outsider among them, and his anger toward his mom has increased recently. The gulf between them feels wider by the day, and Anna feels helpless. Seeing how Daniel struggles and knowing that he feels shame (because he doesn't feel like he belongs) increases Anna's feeling of persistent, intense shame. If we could hear her internal dialogue, we would find she has harsh words for herself. It would probably sound like this:

> *My past marks my life, and it marks Daniel's. It's the scarlet letter for both of us that we can never escape, no matter how much time passes. Daniel will never be whole because of how his life started—with a stupid mom and an immature dad. How could I have ever thought our relationship would be okay when I am the one who caused*

this messed-up situation by getting pregnant as a teenager? He should hate me. I deserve it.

Anna isn't wrestling with whether she is forgiven, which is one doubt that often keeps guilt churning. She believes she is forgiven. She is wrestling with shame because of how her past has "marked," as she said, her life and her son's life. Because of the divorce and an absent father, her son is suffering. The way she sees it, her past now characterizes his life. He's hurting, so she feels shame for this. She caused his pain. A parent never wants to cause pain, so we can understand how shame now churns in Anna.

For parents like Anna who have a moral failure in their past that has had consequences for their children, shame tries to stake its claim on who they are and how they see themselves as parents.

Let's move now to describing the second type of parental shame.

Parents feel shame because something deficient—but not sinful—in their lives has unwanted consequences for their children

Rosalia attends a small church with her husband, eleven-year-old son, and six-year-old daughter. Within their community, there are eight families with school-age children, and all of these families—except Rosalia's—homeschool their kids. Rosalia would have loved to homeschool her kids, but since childhood she has been diagnosed with both dyslexia and attention-deficit disorder (ADD). These two challenges led her and her husband to decide to send their kids to school. But the fact that Rosalia would love to homeschool and isn't doing it because of her dyslexia and ADD causes her shame. The shame makes it challenging for Rosalia to be around the other moms at church because hearing about their homeschooling reminds her of the unwanted difference that exists between her and them. She wonders, *Why am I the only mom who can't do this?* Rosalia hasn't sinned in her decision to send her kids to school. We see that she feels shame for how her bodily based challenges have resulted in a choice that has an impact on her kids. Her unwanted differences mean she can't provide what she longs to give her kids.

We hear, too, how Rosalia is comparing herself to the other moms she knows. Comparison is another trigger for parental shame—wishing we were more like this or that other mom, or longing for the same skills that we see in this or that other dad. We see others who have some quality or resource that blesses their children. And if we don't possess that quality, or if we lack that resource, then that can result in shame. We feel deficient—and we fear that our kids will suffer because of our deficiency. We feel inferior as we compare ourselves to other parents. We know we are supposed to live in community as Christians, but sometimes seeing what other parents are capable of makes us want to hide, so they can't see our incapability. This is another feature of shame: it makes you want to hide—to hide so that others can't see what you lack.

False guilt also can lead to shame. If I have a standard, for example, of what "good" parents provide for their kids and I cannot provide that, then how do I now evaluate myself as a parent? Parents who have lost their jobs, and with them a standard of living that their family has become accustomed to, can feel this shame. Not meeting a financial standard results in false guilt. And this unwanted change economically, with all its impacts on what daily life looks like, now threatens to shape how they see themselves as a parents. *If I can't provide for my family what I always have, then what does that make me? I have failed as a parent.* It is difficult to arrive at a different conclusion after shame like this sets in.

Finally, let's uncover one other major source of shame in parenting.

Parents feel shame because they feel their children's sin or immaturity is a reflection of parental failure

All children (of any age) will experience their own temptations, failures, and struggles. When that inevitably happens, you might feel concerned, or convinced, that you are to blame. When your child's sin is public, then others might judge it as a failure of your parenting, and you might feel shame that you are viewed that way by another person.

The child's failures can range from small to large:

- Frank feels shame when he gets texted to pick up his three-year-old daughter from her Sunday school class—for the second time that month— because she has bitten another child, and the force of the bite broke the child's skin.
- Jason carries shame after his teenage son snuck a bottle of alcohol into their basement during

a hang-out time with his friends. Not only did his son disrespect him to the point of stealing from him and deceiving him afterward, but also others will know about his son's disregard for him and for the rules of his house.

- Ginger and Mario have an adult daughter who is addicted to fentanyl. She has been in and out of rehab since she was seventeen, and her battle with addiction has persisted into her thirties. Ginger and Mario have stopped giving updates to friends and family about how she is doing because there has been no encouraging progress for years. They keep their suffering to themselves and live with the hidden shame that, despite all of their best efforts, they have failed to bring their daughter back from the brink.

From these three examples, we can see, too, that the more intense the struggle for the child, then the greater the risk for intense shame for the parent. We anticipate that Frank could be rid of his shame quite easily if his daughter grows out of the biting stage. But for Ginger and Mario, shame has existed for decades now, made even worse as they've faced numerous people and doctors seeking to understand their daughter's addiction, with some of those people outright accusing them of fault. Their daughter's addiction isn't a stage; it characterizes her life. If Ginger and Mario view themselves as having failed her—their beloved daughter, who is dearer to them than anyone else in this world—then that level of shame has the potential to dominate their lives.

In my years of counseling, I have found that shame is one of the hardest experiences for people to quiet. I think it is because shame is tied up in how we see ourselves. Our individual choices, differences, and experiences as parents come with messages about who we are, and those messages are not easy to ignore.

Even though shame indicts you, let us turn with hope to our Jesus.

QUESTIONS FOR REFLECTION

1. Is there anything in your past that causes you to churn with parental shame?

2. Use the table below to reflect on the causes of whatever shame you listed for question 1. You may list other sources of shame as well.

Moral Failures	Unwanted Differences	Shame from Child's Issue

3. What consequences do you see for your children because of your moral failures and/or unwanted differences? What consequences do you fear for your children because of these?

Chapter 7

HOW JESUS QUIETS SHAME WITH HIS LOVE

When we are ashamed, we are inclined to hide. We discussed this in the last chapter in relation to people, but this inclination to hide is also present in how we relate to God. In fact, the original shame is the kind that exists because of who we are in contrast to who God is. If there is something about who we are that is morally disgraceful, or if we possess an unwanted difference that makes us stand out, or if we feel disgraced by our children's moral failures, then won't we especially feel we should avoid God, who is holy? God is perfect. He is set apart because of how good he is. If we are set apart because of something immoral or deficient, then what can we even expect from him? How can the Holy One be close to us? The whole story of Scripture is about how to resolve this problem. And what we discover is that this is a problem that people cannot resolve. We discover that we are utterly at God's mercy because of our incapability to draw near to a holy God and live in his presence. What will *he* do that will make that possible?

Later in this chapter we will explore how to deal

with shame in parenting, but we have to start with the shame that exists for all of us in our relationship with God. Our most fundamental relationship in life is with God; he is our Creator, and we exist because of him. In him we live, and move, and have our being (Acts 17:28). So if we deal with the shame that exists in other relationships, but fail to deal with the shame in our relationship with God, then we have not experienced the deeper healing that our souls long for. So we will start with how God quiets your shame in your relationship with him and then consider how that healing frees you from the shame you feel in parenting.

So how does God deal with the shame that tells us we should hide from him? To answer this question, let's consider Jesus's earthly mission and ministry.

POWER GOES OUT FROM JESUS

As Jesus begins his public ministry, John baptizes him, and Jesus is immediately driven to the wilderness where he withstands Satan's temptations. After he does, he goes to the synagogue and reads this passage from the prophet Isaiah:

> The Spirit of the Lord is on me,
> Because he has anointed me
> To proclaim good news to the poor;
> He has sent me to proclaim freedom for the
>   prisoners,
> And recovery of sight to the blind,
> To set the oppressed free;
> To proclaim the year of the Lord's favor.
>   (Luke 4:18–19 NIV)

Jesus then sits down and says, "Today this Scripture is fulfilled in your hearing" (Luke 4:21).

To consider how God resolves shame, and how he makes a way for us to come out of hiding, we start here with Jesus's remarkable claim. We learn that Jesus is anointed by the Spirit to perform a specific ministry. The Spirit sends him to preach the gospel, heal the brokenhearted, and liberate the oppressed. And we learn that Jesus is a prophetic figure, as he declares the arrival of this new era: "This Scripture is fulfilled . . . ." Indeed, Jesus proclaims that he brings the full and final fulfillment of God's promise of salvation.[1] He is here. He has come. And salvation, healing, justice, and forgiveness will all come from him and through his ministry. Jesus quickly gets a reputation because of this. People start to flock to him. People come, and they walk away healed. "A great multitude of people" come to "hear Him and be healed of their diseases." Multitudes "tried to touch him, because power was coming from him and healing them all" (Luke 6:17, 19 NKJV).

Notice, in that last verse, that power comes out from Jesus. Power comes *out*. The direction reminds us of our need. We can't conjure up the power to heal ourselves. The power to be healed can't, and won't, come from us. We need power to come from outside of us.

If power goes out from this man, we understand why people in the gospel accounts seek out Jesus. Hearing about Jesus even gives ashamed people the courage to come out of hiding. The "sinful woman"—likely a prostitute—comes to Jesus while he is eating at the house of Simon, a Pharisee (Luke 7). This woman, too, must have heard of Jesus's willingness to help sinners, and so she has come. She comes with a costly amount of oil, and she pours all of it out over Jesus's feet. This is an act of humility and of repentance. She weeps as she washes Jesus's feet with her tears, hair, and oil. We imagine these are tears of joy and relief. She must have known that Jesus would not reject her.

Seeing this spectacle leads Simon to doubt that Jesus is a prophet, because what prophet would let a woman like this touch him and kiss his feet? Jesus perceives his thoughts and launches into a parable. The point of the parable is that those who have been forgiven much will love much. As Jesus concludes his parable, he says that this woman is forgiven. Then he says it to her directly (Luke 7:48).

Think for a moment about what happened. This woman who is known publicly for her sins now receives a public declaration of her forgiveness. Jesus says to her, "Your faith has saved you; go in peace" (Luke 7:50). Her encounter with Jesus ends with sins forgiven, with her shame covered publicly, and with a blessing of peace. An authoritative word has come into her life—and she is now known for something other than her sin. We remember her for something other than her sin.

Ashamed parents also need an authoritative word to come into our lives—a word that can inform our understanding and our interpretations of our lives, of what we have done, and of what we might receive. And when the word comes to us, we only need to practice receiving it, which the messages of shame try to prevent. Shame says, "You are not good enough. You don't deserve to be healed. You don't deserve to be whole." But as we consider Jesus's ministry and what he is here to do, we can see that he comes to give us a new understanding of who we are and of how we are to see ourselves in light of his presence in our lives. Our God is willing to heal us and to forgive us. He has the power to change the narrative about who we are and what we have done. This is the good news of Jesus's ministry. He brings "glad tidings of the kingdom of God" (Luke 8:1 NKJV). Just read through any one of the four gospel accounts and you will see these glad tidings over and over again: Jesus teaches, heals, forgives sins, and then he does it all over again—again and again. He has come to bring glad tidings.

WHEN JESUS HEALS A LEPER

Here's one more story that shows how Jesus lifts shame. This time it involves someone who carries shame not because of a personal sin but because of an unwanted difference—leprosy. Leprosy is an infectious skin disease. If you had this skin disease in Jesus's time, then there was a social stigma attached to it, and sufferers would have experienced social isolation. Moreover, a leper could be deemed ceremonially clean or unclean depending on a priest's assessment of the severity of the disease. This means this person might be kept out of the temple and cut off from worship.

Imagine the shame of living like this:

"Anyone with such a defiling disease [leprosy] must wear torn clothes, let their hair be unkempt, cover the lower part of their face and cry out, 'Unclean! Unclean!' As long as they have the disease they remain unclean. They must live alone; they must live outside the camp." (Leviticus 13:45–46 NIV).

All of this is in the background of a leper who comes to Jesus in Luke 5. In desperation—and in faith—he breaks the Levitical law we just read and seeks Jesus out. The leper falls on his face and implores Jesus, "Lord, if You are willing, You can make me clean" (Luke 5:12 NKJV). You and I already know that Jesus is going to heal him, but let's slow this down so we can more fully appreciate the meaning of the moment. There is so much at stake. All of us who are ashamed should put ourselves in the leper's shoes. We should borrow his words: *Jesus, are you willing? Are you willing to make me well? To deal with the thing about me that is my unwanted difference—the thing that makes me stand out in a way that no one wants to stand out?*

There is a lot at stake for the leper. There is a lot at stake for us. Is Jesus willing? What will he do?

Jesus puts out his hand. He touches the leper, something no one else would have done because of the infectiousness of his disease. But Jesus touches him. And then he speaks: "I am willing; be cleansed" (Luke 5:13 NKJV). The leper is healed.

This is why people flock to Jesus. He is willing to cleanse them. He touches the people no one else would touch.

The question for you then becomes this: Will you join the multitude who flock to Jesus because you know that your healing is in his hands? Will the shamed come to him? Again, thinking about who Jesus is and why he came, this should be the real question: why *wouldn't* I come to him if he is willing to heal me, to help me, and to forgive me? For ashamed people, let's aim for the logic of "He is willing, so *of course* I will come to him." Of course you should come.

But we still haven't quite answered *this* question: How does Jesus quiet our shame?

THE HOLY ONE TAKES OUR SHAME UPON HIMSELF

The answer to that was implicit in the two gospel stories just discussed. But let me make it explicit. The great paradox that unfolds in Jesus's ministry is that as he, the Holy One, brings healing and wholeness to unholy people, he does so by taking shame upon *himself*. At Simon's house, Simon doubted who Jesus was because Jesus let the woman touch and interact with him. Associating himself with her, a known sinner, would bring shame to Jesus. In addition to that, Jesus was already accused of blasphemy for saying he forgives sins (Luke 5:21), so to forgive the woman's sins now is to open himself up to the shame of more false accusations. Jesus does it anyway. Similarly, if Jesus touches the leper, it means he would now be ceremonially unclean because he was in direct contact with the leper's skin. Jesus does it anyway.

It's the same with so many others in the gospel accounts:

- For Jesus to raise Jairus's daughter from the dead, he would have to touch a corpse, which means he would have to take on the shame of becoming ceremonially unclean. He does it anyway.

- When Jesus goes to the house of Zacchaeus, a tax collector whom everyone despises because of his thievery, people complain that Jesus is eating with a sinner. Jesus is shamed by others for his public association with a known sinner. He does it anyway.

Jesus quiets our shame by taking it on himself. He does it again and again. In the events leading up to his death, he endures public mockery and a public beating. People demand he be put to death. He bears the shame of it all. He bears it all the way to the Cross where he dies a shameful and humiliating death.

And this is what we discover:

- Jesus's accumulation of shame delivers the final blow to shame.
- His acts of great mercy come at a great cost to himself—and he willingly pays the cost.
- The Holy One takes on our uncleanness—so that we can be cleansed and made holy.
- Jesus becomes a curse—so that we can inherit God's blessing.
- He dies a shameful death—so that we can live, and live forever.

Starting with his baptism, Jesus publicly identifies himself with sinners. He continues to do—resolutely—throughout his ministry. And he publicly identifies with sinners at his last breath by dying a sinner's death. The sinless one again and again associates himself with sinners—*so that* sinners can become recipients of God's forgiveness.

His accumulation of shame delivers the final blow to shame. As he is dying, he declares, "It is finished." The penalty for sin has been paid. It is accomplished. There is forgiveness now. There is healing now for all who will come to him. Shame is finished, and a new word is spoken over shameful people because of Jesus's work on the cross: "Therefore, if anyone is in Christ, the new creation has come: The old has gone, the new is here! All this is from God, who reconciled us to himself through Christ" (2 Corinthians 5:17–18 NIV).

This new identity is from God. The Creator of heaven and earth makes his people into new creations, and they are new. We need to practice and become really good at believing the authority of God's word about who we are. The messages, feelings, and negative self-talk of shame are so ingrained in how we see ourselves. The messages can be so loud and sound so believable and true. But they aren't what God says. You are a new creation. This is God's authoritative word spoken about you.

In the movie *Wonder*, the main character, Auggie, is a middle-school-aged boy who was born with a severe facial disfigurement. A facial disfigurement is a source of shame; it's an unwanted difference. Auggie has been homeschooled all his life because of his medical needs, but he goes to school for the first time for middle school. We can imagine how difficult it would be at his age to be so obviously different. As you'd sadly expect, kids avoid him and make fun of him.

After enduring this shameful treatment, Auggie comes home and puts on a helmet to cover his face. He's hiding what he feels ashamed of. His mom insists he take it off. He asks her why he has to be so ugly. She says firmly, "You are not ugly, Auggie."

He protests that she is saying that because that's what a mom has to say. And she asks, "Because I'm your mom, it doesn't count?"

"Yes!" he replies.

And she responds, "Because I'm your mom, it counts the most, because I know you the most."[2]

That's the matter of authority.

Whose word counts the most? Whose voice in our life counts the most? Whose view will we agree with? It should be the view of the One who knows us the most and who loves us the most.

The voice who knows you the most says you are a new creation. God's Word counts the most. We don't have to earn this new identity. The Holy One has made us holy—and this is a gift we only have to receive. Author Madeleine L'Engle writes,

> The marvelous thing is that this holiness is nothing we can earn. We don't become holy by acquiring merit badges and brownie points. It has nothing to do with virtue or job descriptions or morality. It is nothing we can *do* in this do-it-yourself world. It is gift, sheer gift, waiting there to be recognized and received. We do not have to be qualified to be holy. We do not have to be qualified to be whole, or healed.[3]

When shame churns, may we recognize and receive the gift of wholeness and healing our God freely offers us.

WHEN THE SON SETS US FREE

In this chapter, I began with the shame that exists in our relationship with God because our most fundamental relationship is with God. He is our Creator, and he is our Redeemer. In redeeming us, he has dealt with our shame and given us a new identity. That is a fundamental truth for you to receive about yourself. It is a sure and certain identity because it comes from God. And from that secure identity he has given you, many applications flow into our parenting. So let's now turn our attention to those applications of how Jesus quiets the shame that we feel as parents.

When we believe and receive the new identity that God has bestowed on us, there is freedom—freedom to be human, which means we are free to admit that we are broken people. We are limited. We are often foolish. We are sinful. But none of this is a cause for shame because of the fundamental identity that God has given us. We can acknowledge that we are still struggling with all that humans struggle with—but without shame, because none of our struggles define us. Do you see the difference? When our struggles and sins define us, then shame sets in. But when God defines our identity, then we are forgiven, redeemed people who still struggle with weakness, limitation, and sin. It's a difference that leads to the freedom to be honest about the fact that we still struggle with weakness, limitation, and sin.

In Anna's case, she can be honest about the real struggles that Daniel is facing because of their family's story. For her to walk in freedom will be to acknowledge something like this to him:

"I know you have been impacted by choices I have made. I know the way our family looks is not what you would have wanted or chosen. I love you, and I am here. You can tell me what you're thinking, feeling, and struggling with. I don't want you to carry your hardships alone."

These are not one-and-done conversations. But they are conversations that would be unlikely to ever happen if Anna was not confident of Christ's certain covering of her shame. It would be too crushing to hear Daniel's pain unless Anna was convinced that Christ defines who she is—not what she did in her past that resulted in pain for her son. But Christ causes her to stand, and therefore, to be emotionally available to Daniel. Christ can help her persevere in finding new ways to pursue Daniel.

Shame can be so crippling. It can stop us from doing something different. It's certainly possible for Daniel's teenage years to pass by with Anna as a mere bystander in his life, seeing his alienation from her only deepen. But if she is free indeed, then she can seek and find the opportunities to be new, to change, in how she relates to him. Any of us can do something new *because* each of us is a new creation. *Who we are now informs what we do now.* This is a reversal of shame. God defines us—and from that identity we go forth and live accordingly.

Not only that, but we get to live *like Christ lived*. Daniel's shame says he is an outsider. But as Anna pursues him, she pushes back against that message, and, by her actions, communicates a new message: "Daniel, you belong—to me, to our family, and to God." In this, she is following the pattern of Christ, who pursued her when she was mired in shame. She gets to embody Christ's love for Daniel, the same love that Christ demonstrated to her. This is the honor that God has shown us in sending his Spirit to be with us: we have the power to be like Christ.

Honesty, humility, seeking and finding new ways of relating and living, and following the pattern of a Savior who covers shame as we cover our children's shame. We move in this direction when we know, deep in our bones, that shame is a problem Jesus decisively dealt with. Shame is finished.

For parents whose shame is because of an unwanted difference that has unwanted impacts on their children, honesty, too, is a balm. Rosalia can be honest with God, honest with herself, honest with her husband, and honest with trusted friends. Admittedly, it is painful to face the real losses that an unwanted difference like Rosalia's brings about. But God's people are not called to grin and bear it. We face real hardships that bring about real losses, and, as we do, God invites us to cry out to him. We don't hold it in. God's people cry. We grieve, and we lament brokenness. These are faithful responses to our hardships as we await God's final redemption when our unwanted differences will cease. We are waiting for that day, and may we wait for it with patience. We can be patient because a full redemption—body and soul—is a sure hope, and we are confident that the God who made the promise will not fail to fulfill it. And we wait with joy because even now our unwanted differences cannot define who we are. They may bring trials and real challenges, but they do not have the authority to define who we are. So we live free from the shame that comes because of our differences, even as we grieve the pain of experiencing them.

For the parents who have a child who is struggling with some kind of failure or challenge, all of the same remedies for shame are also available and relevant. One additional thought for parents to consider is whether they find their identity and ultimate sense of purpose in their children. Many parents unwittingly do this. Another way to come at this question of identity is to consider questions like these: *Where do you find your value and worth? What makes your life meaningful?* If you find your value in your children, or in your success (or failure) as a parent, or in your child's successes (or failures), then these are the wrong places to find your life's meaning. Maybe it can go well for a time if your child is doing well, or if you perceive yourself as a very fine parent. But if the inverse becomes true, and your children's folly reflects your failure, it can be crushing and induce shame.

So as another remedy, search your heart: Do you find your identity in your children, in who they are, or in how they're doing? Of course, being a parent is part of who you are. But at your core, is it where you derive value and worth? If you do, then please recognize that to build your fundamental sense of yourself on your role as a parent is to build it on shifting sand. It will not support you in any lasting way, because it is not designed to do so. If you struggle here, then this is an area where you can commit to seeing yourself as God does. God established your value and worth when he made you a son or daughter in his family. You are a son. You are a daughter. You are a child of the Triune God. He alone has the authority to tell you who you are, and you are primarily defined by your connection to him. Your identity in him is a reality that doesn't change, because God established it. This is what helps parents come out of hiding from shame when our children have morally failed.

Notice how each of the parents from the previous chapter come out of hiding. They do so in ways that balance honesty, concern, and a desire to honor their children's reputations with appropriate disclosures.

Frank can humbly go to the other child's parents to check on how the bite mark is healing. He can reach out to his pediatrician and ask for advice on how he can help his daughter. He can be firm and clear with his instruction to his daughter, patiently teaching her what loving and kind behavior toward others looks like.

Jason can contact the parents of his son's friends and confess his serious error in keeping alcohol in an accessible location. Moving forward, he can commit to locking any alcohol in a cabinet until his son matures and rebuilds the trust he broke so that his son understands the weightiness of what he did and the risks he took to his and his friends' safety. Jason can discipline his son in age-appropriate ways.

Again, the messages of shame say, "Hide. Don't tell anyone about your child's struggle. Keep it in the dark so you're not exposed." But God's people live in the light—Jesus beckons us to come out of hiding—and as we come, he equips us to live constructively amidst struggle. Frank and Jason are invited to live constructively.

It is the same for Ginger and Mario. They are hurting. They are vulnerable to despair, and this, too, keeps them closed off from others. They think, *Who would want to be close to two brokenhearted people like us?* But strength and success are not prerequisites to be a member of Christ's body. God made them members, and it is the privilege of the other members to care for those who are hurting. For a long-lasting suffering like theirs, constructive living involves openness to share how they're really doing, what they're really struggling with, how their faith is weak, how their trust is waning, and what their fears are. And constructive living involves openness to do so with trusted individuals who will keep their confidences out of respect for their daughter and her unfolding story. They need the words and prayers of God's people to combat shame's insidious messages, so how can they position themselves to receive care for the hard days ahead?

To close, we have seen that no matter the source of our shame, God has forged a path for our freedom. In Zephaniah 3:19, God says he brings his people praise and honor in every land where they suffered shame. That is a promise for restoration in every place shame touches our lives. This merciful God honors ashamed people. He has honored you with the gift of a new identity.

Jesus quiets shame by saying that you are a new creation. Trust this word, because his voice counts the most.

QUESTIONS FOR REFLECTION

1. Think about Jesus saying that power went out from him. Where do you need his power right now?

2. Who you are now informs what you can do now. Because of Jesus's word spoken into our lives about who we are, we don't have to be paralyzed by shame. We can come out of hiding. We can take small steps of love. Are there any ways or places you can come out of hiding? What would that look like?

3. Are there any small steps of love you can take toward your children? What might they look and sound like?

A PRAYER FOR ASHAMED PARENTS

God, I long to be free from shame.

Thank you that I am free indeed. Help me to receive the gift of that truth by faith.

Help me grow in trusting that your words about me count the most.

Help me live according to who I am in you.

Chapter 8

REGRETS IN PARENTING

Regret is the final distressing experience that we will cover. When we struggle with regret, we review and rehearse choices that we have made. If we were somehow involved or played a role in a consequential matter, then we review and rehearse what we did in that matter. Usually we get caught up in this reviewing and rehearsing when there has been an unwanted outcome. For parents who struggle with regret, it's when we see an unwanted outcome in our children's lives, or there is an unwanted dynamic in our relationship with them. It's a churn that loops around and around.

Regrets tend to loop like this: *what I did, what I wish I had done, what I did, what I wish I had done.*

Then our imaginations enter the loop—imagining what would be better if I had done what I wish I had done. But then I remember what I actually did, and the loop starts all over again:

> *What I did, what I wish I had done, how things would be better if I had done what I wish I had done.*

What I did, what I wish I had done, how things would be better if I had done what I wish I had done.

And when we see that there is something we could have done, but didn't do at the time, we might struggle with self-loathing or self-blame. When we see that there has been a missed opportunity to have an impact that we wanted, then we have harsh words for ourselves or harsh feelings toward ourselves.

Daniel and Cassidy are caught up in regret. When their two daughters were in their early teens, Daniel accepted a job in a different state and uprooted the family from a medium-sized suburban town where they were well connected to a small-sized city where they knew no one. The differences were immense. While Daniel and Cassidy struggled to reestablish themselves and find their footing in a new city, they unintentionally overlooked their girls' struggles with the move. As the daughters made new connections at school, this formerly close family of four began to drift from one another. When their older daughter started attending political rallies with her friends and identified herself as an activist, it was a wake-up call for Daniel and Cassidy as they realized that they had neglected their girls in this transition. Who were their girls now? What were their friends like? What had happened to their close family unit? Now they felt almost like strangers to each other.

As they considered questions like these, the loop of regrets started to go around and around. Though it was understandable that they had been overwhelmed with all the changes from the move, they still needed to shepherd their girls through the transition. Was it too late? What now?

Let's hear one more story that further underscores the distress of parental regret.

Henry is a fifty-seven-year-old father of four adult children—and Henry is a new believer. He was raised in the church, but he had not pursued a life of faith as an adult. But after his wife's unexpected death, he had a faith awakening. He is now involved in a local church and growing in his knowledge and love of Scripture. As he fellowships with other believers and gets to know fellow parents, he has begun to struggle with regret about how he and his wife raised their children. Though they provided a loving, stable home, they did not teach them about the Christian faith or bring them to church. Though Henry's children have grown to have stable lives themselves, not one of them is a believer.

Henry has also realized just how much he depended on his wife to maintain a relationship with his kids. Without her there, Henry can see that he doesn't actually know how to relate to them. Quiet and passive temperamentally, Henry tries to recall how he related to them when they were children, but he only remembers the ways he hung back and relied on his wife to do the relational and emotional work.

Along with these upsetting realizations, Henry keeps rehearsing his own upbringing—his believing grandparents and parents who nurtured him and taught him about the Lord. He asks himself, *Why didn't I carry that on with my own kids?* Over and over again, he goes back to when he began to drift in his faith in his late teen years, searching for an answer to that question. Over and over, he recalls his children's years at home—the music lessons, the sports teams, and the summer camps. These were all good things he and his wife provided, but they didn't include the best thing—a connection to the living God and a connection to his people.

Though Henry also wishes for his own sake, and for the sake of his marriage, that he would have had this faith awakening much earlier in life, his regrets loop around how the timing impacted how he parented and raised his kids. And this is usually the case for parents. They are less concerned with choices they have made that come at a cost that they themselves have to bear. They are more concerned when their kids bear the cost in some way—and that is where their regret fixates.

Like Henry, many parents whose kids are grown struggle with regret. The "empty nest" is a quiet nest with newfound space and time to ponder the years that have gone by. One of the most repeated phrases I've heard about parenting is this: "the days are long, but the years are short." This phrase refers to the "short" years we have when the children are in our homes and under our roof. This is the season of parenting when we have a significant opportunity to shape and influence our children and the direction of their lives. And while this phrase captures something that resonates with the experience of many parents, it also induces a lot of anxious thoughts: *Time is slipping away! You only have so many chances! Don't blow it!* Then, once the children are out of the family home, we agree that the years were indeed short. *How time flies! What did we do with those years? Did we make the most of them?* It seems our opportunity for the most influence has passed. There is no going back. So when we review what we made of those short years, how did we do?

If we were to ask ourselves that question and make accurate self-evaluations, we'd all find a mix of true guilt and false guilt. Both can lead to regrets. And if we define ourselves by those failures, then shame will also be in the mix of that churn. Our previous discussions on guilt and shame are, therefore, relevant as we consider regret, but let us now turn with faith to learn specifically how Jesus quiets our regrets with his love.

QUESTIONS FOR REFLECTION

1. Though the parents in this chapter have older children, parents with younger children can also struggle with regret. The regrets can cover a range from big to small decisions, such as a mom who regrets ending breastfeeding "too soon," or a dad who regrets missing his son's playoff game because he was at work. From big ones to small ones, what regrets do you have in parenting?

2. How does your "regret loop" prevent you from moving forward in ways you'd like to move forward as a parent?

Chapter 9

HOW JESUS QUIETS REGRETS WITH HIS LOVE

We'll begin with a story. It's a story that Jesus tells that you are likely familiar with. But consider it again in light of your own regrets in your parenting.

In Luke 15, Jesus is teaching, and tax collectors and sinners gather to listen. Seeing the kind of crowd that Jesus attracts, some Pharisees and teachers of the law mutter, "See, this man welcomes sinners and eats with them" (Luke 15:2 NIV). Jesus doesn't directly respond to their comments, but begins to tell parables. The third of these is the parable of the prodigal son.

Here is how Jesus tells the story:

"There was a man who had two sons. The younger one said to his father, 'Father, give me my share of the estate.' So he divided his property between them.

Not long after that, the younger son got together all he had, set off for a distant country and there squandered his wealth in wild living.

After he had spent everything, there was a severe famine in that whole country, and he began to be in need. So he went and hired himself out to a citizen of that country, who sent him to his fields to feed pigs. He longed to fill his stomach with the pods that the pigs were eating, but no one gave him anything.

When he came to his senses, he said, 'How many of my father's hired servants have food to spare, and here I am starving to death! I will set out and go back to my father and say to him: Father, I have sinned against heaven and against you. I am no longer worthy to be called your son; make me like one of your hired servants.' So he got up and went to his father." (Luke 15:11–20a NIV)

Let me pause the story and make a few comments. First, the son's request for his share of the estate prior to his father's death would be deeply offensive in this culture. Second, the fact that there was an estate indicates this family's wealth. The son is provided for, so his request is about himself and his desire for "wild living." After a period of squandering his wealth and wild living, he is left with nothing. He must resort to hiring himself out. He is so hungry he envies a pig's food! Third, he regrets where his choices have brought him. If he didn't feel regret, then he would have continued on where he was and tried to make it work. But instead, he "comes to his senses" and heads home. He feels regret, and then he has a choice

to make. Will he turn toward his father, or make a
choice that results in more harm—a choice like self-
pity, self-disgust, wallowing, or denial of his wrong-
doing? He chooses well.

After he repents and heads toward home, the question becomes: How will the father respond to his son's
homecoming? The son anticipates that he will become
a servant in his father's house, but will not be restored
to his rights as a son. To him, that seems just given his
offense against his father.

Let's see what the father does.

> But while he was still a long way off, his father
> saw him and was filled with compassion for
> him; he ran to his son, threw his arms around
> him and kissed him.
>
> The son said to him, "Father, I have sinned
> against heaven and against you. I am no longer
> worthy to be called your son." But the father
> said to his servants, "Quick! Bring the best
> robe and put it on him. Put a ring on his finger
> and sandals on his feet. Bring the fattened calf
> and kill it. Let's have a feast and celebrate. For
> this son of mine was dead and is alive again; he
> was lost and is found." So they began to cele-
> brate. (Luke 15:20b–24 NIV)

The son discovers that his father is even more gracious than he imagined. What a surprise welcomes
him! The picture Jesus gives us in the story is so sweet.
The father longs for his son, even after his son has been
so foolish. The father has not stopped loving him and

is, in fact, waiting for him, hoping his son would return home. Jesus says that when the father sees his son, he has compassion on him. He runs toward him, embraces him, and kisses him. The son confesses and seeks his forgiveness, but notice in Jesus's telling of this story that the father doesn't even respond to his son's confession. He doesn't scold him or tell him that he has been so hurt by what he's done. He doesn't tell him how worried he was, or how miserable it was not knowing where he was or if he was safe. Instead, the father speaks to the servants. He asks them to bring out the robe, ring, and sandals and to get a calf to eat in celebration. The best robe is a mark of distinction. The ring signifies authority. The shoes signify the status of a free man, because servants did not wear shoes. And the fattened calf was for special occasions only. These gifts bestowed on the son indicate a full restoration of the son to the father. The father has completely and fully forgiven his son, and they celebrate.

The Pharisees muttered that Jesus welcomes sinners and eats with them. To that, we say, "That's only the half of it! He welcomes sinners into his own arms, kisses them, and makes them sons and daughters of the Most High King!"

Put yourself in the son's shoes because this is the story you and I are now a part of. Let's learn what the son learned about his father: the way back home is always open and the Father is waiting with open arms. In light of this reality, there is hope in the face of regrets.

Here then are two takeaways when we struggle with regrets in parenting. First, in the face of our folly, let's come to our senses and make our way back to the

Father. Second, let's remember God is even more gracious than we imagine him to be.

When we churn with regrets, the loop goes around and around. God is absent from that loop. But to come to our senses is to remember that in my story, I am not the only one who exists in it. It's not just me, what I have done, and what I wish I had done. There is a gracious Father waiting for us to turn to him and receive his embrace. How hard it is to recognize that we would have liked to have done something differently in our parenting, but missed an opportunity! To struggle with regrets is a kind of suffering. It is truly painful to see our missteps. But even if our own foolish choices have resulted in unwanted outcomes related to our children, to come to our senses is to turn toward our heavenly Father and to head toward him. It is to receive the comfort of his embrace, to receive the comfort of his forgiveness, and to receive his comfort for how we feel about our choices. He comforts us because he is compassionate toward us.

If you think about people in the Bible who might have wrestled with regrets, the apostle Paul would be a prime candidate. He was an enemy of the early Christians and he actively sought to eliminate the growth of the church. But he had an encounter with Jesus, and, like all who meet Jesus, he walked away a changed person. God chose an enemy of the church and used him to prove that Jesus is the Messiah (Acts 9:22). And Paul walked in that calling. Regrets keep us looking backward. But Paul himself chose to press forward—and so we don't hear from him that he carries regrets. Listen to what he says:

> I press on to take hold of that for which Christ Jesus took hold of me. Brothers and sisters, I do not consider myself yet to have taken hold of it. But one thing I do: Forgetting what is behind and straining toward what is ahead, I press on toward the goal to win the prize for which God has called me heavenward in Christ Jesus. (Philippians 3:12–14 NIV)

This is not a man consumed with regrets because of his past sins and failures. The life, death, and resurrection of Jesus have gripped him and rearranged how he thinks about his life. We learn that life in Jesus is pressing forward. It's looking ahead because we are a heaven-bound people. What we've done or failed to do in our past can't change that, so we leave it behind and press on toward the goal, the prize God has called us to. We are a people who look ahead.

Press on, dear parents. The story of your parenting isn't over. Jesus took hold for you a life in him that is empowered by his Spirit (John 14:16–17). His Spirit is with us, making all things new in us. Take hold of that life. In the Spirit's power, we are a people who strain toward what is ahead.

Pressing on can be beautifully expressed in so many ways! For Daniel and Cassidy, there are many responses that honor God and what he has done for them in Christ. Pressing on can look like this:

- Accepting the limitations that come from both being human, and from finding themselves overwhelmed in the midst of a massive move.

- Praying for the Lord to identify the areas of true failure in how they parented their daughters. It's not a moral failure for them to struggle amid all the upheaval of a major relocation, but were there ways they sinned against their girls in how they responded to, or failed to respond to, the changes?
- Confessing any true sins and failures to their daughters and seeking their forgiveness.
- Inviting their daughters to share with them how they may have felt hurt by them—by either the choice to move or how they navigated the move—and remaining open to hearing from them about this in the future.
- Grieving together as a couple for the losses that they have faced in the move. They said good-bye to their church family and numerous dear friends. They can honestly acknowledge their losses and lament them.
- Choosing to trust God for the timing of the move, which is a difficult time to introduce such a significant change in the lives of adolescents.
- Committing to pursuing their daughters relationally, to jumping back into their lives right away, to prioritizing family dinners, to inviting their friends to their home so they can get to know them, to asking questions about their girls' new friends, such as, what do they like about them?
- Committing to expressing honest concern when appropriate about their girls' new friends and

the influence that they see, and helping their daughters grow in wise discernment about what makes a good friend. In connection with their older daughter's "activism," helping her think through questions like these: What makes a cause worthy of our devotion? What concerns her about the issues she's become passionate about? What does responsible political involvement look like?

- Committing to finding a church together and to attending regularly as a family.
- Committing to praying for their daughters.

Each of these is a version of pressing on. Each is a straining toward that which Jesus has taken hold of for his people.

For Henry, too, there are so many options. How can he press on? By making choices like these:

- Sharing with his children his story of how his faith renewal came about.
- Confessing his failure to God and to his children to raise them in the church and have a Christ-centered home, and asking their forgiveness for this.
- Confessing to God and to his children that he was relationally negligent and relied on his wife to do the relational work.
- Committing to getting to know his kids now, pursuing time with them, and looking for ways to be engaged in their lives. Being honest with

his community of trusted friends when he feels overwhelmed by getting to know his four kids better.

- Confessing any temptations to revert back to relational disengagement, because it is what is familiar to him.
- Inviting his children to church with him. If they say no, finding winsome ways to pursue them spiritually.
- Letting them know he is open to their questions about the Christian faith and open to any ongoing conversation that his faith renewal raises for them.
- Praying for his children's faith.
- Choosing to trust God for the timing of his faith renewal.

TRUSTING GOD WITH THE TIMING

Both lists included trusting God with the timing. For Daniel and Cassidy, it is with the timing of the move that happened at a vulnerable stage of their girls' development, and for Henry, it is with the timing of his faith renewal. Let me speak on this matter of timing, because it is easy to say, "trust God with how life unfolds," but it is not easy to do—especially when it involves a high-stakes matter regarding our kids. I totally understand that. So if you struggle to trust, what's a way forward? When we are struggling to trust God, we may need to wrestle with him. We should bring him the hard questions on our hearts about the timing. Ask him why. Ask him why not. Tell him you don't get why the story has played out so far the way it has. God is open to that kind of honesty and wrestling—and if we are struggling to trust him, then start there with him. He is more gracious than you imagine.

A related struggle with God's timing is with the pace at which he grows and sanctifies us. Again, this is especially hard to accept when our level of spiritual maturity has an unwanted impact on our kids—and regrets follow.

> *If I had the wisdom back then that I have now, I would have done things so much differently with my kids.*
> *If I had experienced this growth in my character earlier, then I could have been such a better model to my kids.*

We hear hints of both these regrets in Daniel's, Cassidy's, and Henry's stories. We believe God is the author and perfecter of our faith, and when he perfects us more slowly than we'd like—and our kids suffer for it—then we struggle with him in this. Wouldn't it be nice if he hurried up and perfected us? I long for my kids to know me as a fully redeemed mom! For their sake, I wish I could relate to them perfectly and have perfect patience, all wisdom, and sound guidance, always and at all times. But it's not who I am—not even close. *Why not, God?!*

It is maddening at times that he could change me faster than he does. For some reason, he is content to transform me into Jesus's image over time. In the face of that reality, I discover a call to submit to his timing. We are the clay and he is our potter—and when and how he chooses to remake us is in his hands (Isaiah 64:8). Submitting and trusting him in this isn't easy. I've said that already, but it bears repeating. When I am struggling to trust him, it helps to remember that I am not doing so as an act of blind faith. He has already given me good reasons to trust him. Instead of looking at my past, I look at his. What has *he* already done? What is in God's past? I always come back to this: "If God is for us, who can be against us? He who did not spare his own Son, but gave him up for us all—how will he not also, along with him, graciously give us all things?" (Romans 8:31–32 NIV).

Long ago, before any of your failures or mistakes, God already did something that would change your life and that contained the power to rearrange the trajectory of your life story. Let that astounding reality soften your heart toward him when you doubt his timing. To cast our reasons to trust in Romans 8 language, by faith, we can affirm what follows:

- I choose to trust God because he is for me. He is for my children.
- I choose to trust God because he did not spare his own Son, but gave him up for me. He gave his Son up for my children.
- I choose to trust God because he is a gracious giver—even giving his Son to me. He graciously gives his Son to me and to my children.

Notice I said "choose" here and in the bulleted lists earlier. That is because we can choose to trust even when we don't like God's timing, wish it had been different, or don't understand why it is the way it is. We choose to trust because he has given reasons to trust, and he is the same yesterday, today, and forever, so he won't fail us now. If you're still bothered with his timing in changing you, then bother him about it. Wrestle with him about it. And press on. Keep growing. Keep depending on him for your growth. He will not fail you.

Some parents might need to extend this same faith into trusting God with the timing of their children's spiritual growth. If you're one of these parents, consider Henry again: he would face a strong pull to imagine his kids as committed Christians now if only he had made different choices back then, when they were young. But is their story in his hands? Is it all up to him? Of course not. Our God is still the potter in his children's lives, and God can fashion all of the details from what has transpired so far in their story into a beautiful new creation. It's who he is and it's what he does. And so we must come back to this: he has given us good reasons to trust him. So, like Jairus, run to Jesus with what is most precious to you—your children and your hopes for their well-being and safekeeping—and ask him to tend to them. May your faith rise as you remember how Jesus hurried to Jairus's house. He cares about our kids. He is the same yesterday, today, and forever—and he won't fail them now.

To gather together all of the biblical testimony we have covered in this chapter, this is the conclusion we come to: Jesus quiets regrets by helping us come to our senses and run to his open embrace. He comforts our sorrows for what happened in the past. Gently, he encourages us, "You can trust me with all that has happened. Trust me with your children. Now press on—keep going—because I am in your midst and I am mighty to save."

The churn of regrets is a loop that circles around and around and goes nowhere. But life in Christ breaks you free from that loop. God sets you on a path. You have a direction to go—and you will have his help along the way. Press on in your parenting today in the power of the Spirit.

QUESTIONS FOR REFLECTION

1. Something you might have heard in jest, but that carries a bit of truth, is parents saying they will have to pay for their kid's therapy one day. It's a way for them to acknowledge on some level that their issues do (or could) cause hurt for their kids. Imagine you have an adult child who comes to you and says, "I want to talk to you about some ways I have been hurt by you." As you reflect on this chapter, what would you hope to say in response?

2. If your children shared their hurts, how might Christ help you hear real ways you harmed your children? What specifically would you call to mind about Jesus's heart that would bring comfort?

3. Write a list of what pressing on could look like in any area where you have regrets in parenting.

4. Read Philippians 4:4–8. What does Paul encourage believers to do and to think about, and how could it help you in your thoughts when you are caught up in a regret loop? What can you practice?

A PRAYER FOR PARENTS WITH REGRETS

Help me to trust you, God, with what I would
    have done differently.

Comfort me in your embrace.

Thank you that I can press on, with your help
    and in your power.

Help me to do that.

Conclusion

GLADNESS MULTIPLIED

The Lord your God is in your midst,
a mighty one who will save;
he will rejoice over you with gladness;
he will quiet you by his love;
he will exult over you with loud singing.
(Zephaniah 3:17)

One of the reasons I chose the book of Zephaniah and have repeated the use of "Jesus quiets" is because it's a parental image. The churn is a distressing experience for us. And so think about when your child is in distress. Imagine they are crying out to you because something is wrong. They need your help, your intervention, and your attention. What do you do? You come close, and you soothe them. You comfort them. You quiet their cries by attending to their pain, and by being a presence who is there to relieve their suffering. This is who Jesus is to you. Just as you would say to your child, "Shh, it's okay. Shh, I'm here. Shh, it's going to be all right," so Jesus draws near to attend to you. And with him there with us, in our midst, everything really will be okay. Everything will really be all right.

There is no equivalent to Jesus drawing near to us. No one can make the kind of difference that Jesus of Nazareth makes when he comes close. He is God. It is God who comes close to you to quiet you. Receive the comfort of his embrace—again and again.

You might object to the idea of being like a child before the Lord. To be like a child is to be weak. Yes, that's right. But the Bible's logic is this: when we are weak, then we are strong. Weakness is a characteristic of God's children. He made us to be dependent upon him. He is the mighty one who saves. We are not. He is the strong one, so let him rescue you—again and again. The kingdom of God is for "such as these," for those who are childlike in their dependence on their Father and who know their need of him. There is no shame, then, when we see our need. Only be like a child, and run to him.

I also like the language of "quiets" because it doesn't suggest that the churn goes away altogether. None of the churns any of us face in life will completely stop until the day we see our Jesus face-to-face. Yet he still comes close now. He comes close today, and he has real impact—a quieting impact—on your parental churn. I am making this point because I don't want you to walk away from this book with a new standard to hold yourself to that sounds something like, "Now that I have taken time to consider how Jesus helps my emotional distress in parenting, I shouldn't struggle anymore." I don't want that to become a new, self-imposed standard you carry, only to find yourself churning with false guilt because you are struggling with how you see yourself as a parent! Please be careful of that. Instead, when you are struggling, imagine him as that comforting parent. As you bring your distress to him, imagine him drawing close to you and gently saying to you, "Shh, shh. I am here." Let him speak. Quiet down and listen. Over and over again, hear what he says.

- "I care about you." (1 Peter 5:7)
- "I use my power on your behalf." (Luke 8:46)
- "Fear me." (Matthew 10:28)
- "Humble yourself before me by placing your trust in me. I am in control."(James 4:6–10)
- "My grace is sufficient in your weakness." (2 Corinthians 12:9)
- "You are a new creation." (2 Corinthians 5:17)
- "Run to me. I will embrace you." (Luke 15:20)
- "Press on." (Philippians 3:12–14)

These are the words that count the most because the one who said them loves you the most. Behold your God, and see how much he loves you. He quiets you because he delights in you. You picked up this book feeling like a failure. Set it down having believed and received the word that he is singing over you. He *exults* over you, and that means he is joyful and exuberant about who you are. You bring gladness to your heavenly Father. That is who you are.

These are glad tidings that have come to you from Jesus Christ. Receive and believe them with gladness and with the utmost confidence because the one who has spoken them is trustworthy and true.

QUESTIONS FOR REFLECTION

1. How are you comforted by knowing Jesus wants to quiet you with his love?

2. How can you become increasingly comfortable with seeing yourself as a dependent child who looks to your Father for what you need? What is challenging about seeing yourself like that and acting that way with God? How is it comforting?

3. Take some time and look up the Bible verses referenced that are the Lord's voice to you. Which ones are particularly comforting to you? Write down one or two and make them your daily prayer.

ACKNOWLEDGMENTS

To get a book to publication is a collective effort, and I'm deeply grateful for those who have helped along the way. Thank you to the New Growth Press team for your investment in me and this book. Thank you to my colleagues who shape my thinking and my ministry daily—and special thanks to Darby Strickland and Mike Emlet who in particular helped me shape this content. Thank you to my church community who was excited about this book and prayed me through the writing process. Thank you to my consultation group, my insightful sounding board and enthusiastic encouragers: Julie Lowe, Jackie Snider, Jamie Yoo, Kïrsten Christianson, and Christy Edwards. And most of all, thank you to my dearest ones at home—my husband, Chad, who is ever-supportive, and my two darling children. Every day, the three of you give grace to me and love me without reserve. You remind me of what Jesus is like. I love you forever and ever!

ENDNOTES

Chapter 1

1. @daddygofish, "My wife and I didn't renew our vows, but we did solve our third grader's math problem together," Twitter (X) post, January 30, 2024, https://twitter.com/daddygofish/status/1752545966195134840

2. @maryfairybobrry, "My favorite part about talking to my teens is when they give me direct eye contact, listen intently, nod understandingly, and then take out their AirPods when I finish and say, 'huh?'" Twitter (X) post, https://twitter.com/maryfairybobrry/status/1750217975494320342

3. William T. Sleeper, "Jesus, I Come," 1887.

Chapter 4

1. I have also written on this topic. See Lauren Whitman, *Mom Guilt: Escaping Its Strong Hold* (Greensboro, NC: New Growth Press, 2022).

2. Sharon Hays, *The Cultural Contradictions of Motherhood* (New Haven, CT: Yale University Press, 1996), 8.

3. According to the American Time Use Survey, cited in Jennifer Senior, *All Joy and No Fun: The Paradox*

of Modern Parenthood (New York, NY: Harper-Collins Publishers, 2015), 122.

4. Senior, *All Joy and No Fun*, 152.

5. Senior, *All Joy and No Fun*, 154.

6. Senior, *All Joy and No Fun*, 159–160.

Chapter 5

1. Malcolm Guite, *Sounding the Seasons: Poetry for the Christian Year, or Sounding the Seasons: Seventy Sonnets for the Christian Year* (Canterbury Press, Norfolk, UK: 2012), 53.

2. Andrew Bonar, *Memoir and Remains of R.M. M'Cheyne* (Carlisle, PA: Banner of Truth, 1966), 293.

Chapter 7

1. Insights from Darrell L. Bock, *Luke NIV Application Commentary* (Grand Rapids, MI: Zondervan Academic, 1996), 134–138.

2. *Wonder*, directed by Stephen Chboksy, based on the 2012 book *Wonder* by R. J. Palacio (Lionsgate, 2017). 1 hr., 53 min.

3. Madeleine L'Engle, *Walking on Water: Reflections on Faith and Art* (New York, NY: Convergent Books, 2016), 49.

ccef

CCEF is committed to restoring Christ to counseling and counseling to the church. They seek to accomplish this mission through resources, courses, events, and counseling.

To learn more or explore CCEF's resources, visit **ccef.org**.